Quiet Water

Canoe Guide

New Hampshire
Vermont

Also Available from the Appalachian Mountain Club

AMC River Guides
Maine
Massachusetts/Connecticut/Rhode Island
New Hampshire/Vermont

New England White Water River Guide
Ray Gabler

White Water Handbook
John T. Urban, revised by T. Walley Williams

River Rescue
Les Bechdel and Slim Ray

AMC Trail Guides
Guide to Mt. Desert Island and Acadia National Park
Guide to Mt. Washington and the Presidential Range
Hiking the Mountain State (West Virginia)
Maine Mountain Guide
Massachusetts and Rhode Island Trail Guide
North Carolina Hiking Trails
White Mountain Guide

Short Hikes & Ski Trips Around Pinkham Notch
A Day Tripper's Guide to the Mt. Washington Area
Linda Buchanan Allen

Founded in 1876, the Appalachian Mountain Club, a non-profit organization with 50,000 members, promotes the protection, enjoyment, and wise use of the open spaces, rivers, mountains and forests of the Northeast.

For more information or details about membership in the AMC, write to the Appalachian Mountain Club, 5 Joy Street, Boston, MA 02108; or call 617-523-0636.

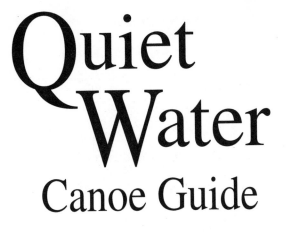

APPALACHIAN MOUNTAIN CLUB

Quiet Water

Canoe Guide

New Hampshire
Vermont

BEST PADDLING LAKES AND PONDS
FOR ALL AGES

Alex Wilson

APPALACHIAN MOUNTAIN CLUB BOOKS
BOSTON, MASSACHUSETTS

Cover Photographs: Hanson Carroll, Stephen Gorman
Other Photographs: Alex Wilson
Cartography: Nadav Malin, West River Communications, Inc. Brattleboro, Vermont
Wildlife Illustrations: Cathy Johnson
Book Design: Carol Bast Tyler

Distributed by The Talman Company

Library of Congress Cataloging-in-Publication Data

Wilson, Alex, 1955–
    Appalachian Mountain Club quiet water canoe guide : New Hampshire, Vermont : best paddling lakes and ponds for all ages / Alex Wilson.
        p. cm.
    Includes index.
    ISBN 1–878239–14–7 (alk. paper)
    1. Canoes and canoeing—New Hampshire—Guidebooks. 2. Canoes and canoeing—Vermont—Guidebooks. 3. New Hampshire—Description and travel—1981– —Guidebooks. 4. Vermont—Description and travel—1981– —Guidebooks. I. Title. II. Title: Quiet water canoe guide.
GV776.N4W55   1992
797.1'22'099742—dc20   92–4968
                                                   CIP

Contents

Introduction

Quiet water is something special. As an avid paddler, I've always sought those out-of-the-way lakes and ponds—places where you can leave for a few hours or a few days the hustle and bustle of everyday life; where you can watch white clouds dance behind wild majestic mountains, fly-cast for trout in the early morning mist, or listen to the wild and haunting cry of the loon. I first fell in love with quiet water canoeing as a boy, camping with my parents in central Vermont, New York's Adirondack Park, and Algonquin Provincial Park in Ontario. We would rent a canoe and paddle about in the little protected coves of the lakes we camped on, and I'd learn about the plants and animals we saw there. This love for quiet water canoeing has stayed with me—and grown—now that I'm the parent teaching my children about the outdoors.

In the years since childhood I've been keeping an eye out for quiet water canoeing locations. When I moved to southern Vermont in 1980 and set about exploring the area, I searched through all the boating literature I could find. I discovered some excellent canoe books, but they were all guides to river canoeing—nothing on lakes and ponds. Using road maps, I began exploring the area—first alone and later with a family—and discovered some wonderful spots. When an opportunity arose to assemble a guide to quiet water canoeing for the Appalachian Mountain Club, my explorations spread out and became more systematic. I spent late evenings poring over maps. I drove thousands of miles, and spent dozens of nights camped in a tent—often with my wife and young daughters—exploring New Hampshire and Vermont. What I found is shared in the pages of this book.

From more than nine hundred lakes and ponds in New Hampshire and Vermont, sixty-two have been selected for inclusion—places that I especially like. The book describes how to get there, where you can park, camping opportunities in the area (in most cases), and, most important, what's special about the lake or pond and what you might see there.

Especially if you have to drive long distances to reach a lake or pond, this book will give you an idea of what to expect and help you avoid disappointment or unrealistic expectations. There are a lot of lakes and ponds, for example, that seem way out in the middle of nowhere, yet are either heavily developed, full of motorboats, or less enticing to the quiet water paddler for some other reason. With this guide, you can spend your precious weekends or vacation enjoying paddling—instead of driving around to find an acceptable place after a lake that looked great on the road map turns out to be wall-to-wall motorboats and summer homes.

Unlike books on river canoeing, this guide does not need to devote a lot of space to warnings about rapids or how to plan a day's travel around put-in and take-out locations. With lake and pond canoeing, it's usually a lot simpler: you park your car, load up the canoe, paddle around as long as you wish, and then return to the car. In a sense then, this is a book about the ends, not the means—what you will see and why you might want to visit a body of water.

How These Lakes and Ponds Were Selected

This guide is obviously a selective listing of only a small percentage of the lakes and ponds in the two states. I started the selection process with some definite prejudices when it comes to canoeing. I had a good idea of what I like in a lake or pond: pretty scenery; not too much development around the shoreline (totally undeveloped lakes and ponds are best, but a book on these places in New Hampshire and Vermont would be very short); not too many motorboats; a varied shoreline with lots of coves and inlets to explore; and interesting plants, animals, and geological formations.

I wanted to include a variety of types of bodies of water in the book: some big lakes for when you really want to cover a lot of distance, and some small protected ponds that are just right for young paddlers and short excursions, or when it's windy. To make the book useful to more people, I tried to include as much of New Hampshire and Vermont as possible, though I admit there are more destinations in the far-northern reaches of the two states than elsewhere. You just can't beat some of these distant lakes and ponds!

I had a bunch of favorites when I took on this project, but I knew that I'd be exploring lakes and ponds I had never even heard of, let alone paddled on. Finding the nicest would take some work. I asked friends and friends of friends—anyone I could find who had an interest in quiet water canoeing—for suggestions. They proved a big help, but I went still further, spending days poring over maps, including the large-format DeLorme Atlases of New Hampshire and Vermont. With these and U.S. Geological Survey topographical maps, I could get a sense of how developed a lake or pond was (although, as I quickly found out, some of these maps are considerably out of date when it comes to showing development).

I compiled an initial list of about a hundred lakes and ponds to visit, and that list expanded to around 120 as I learned of other spots during my research. After hundreds of miles of paddling, I narrowed these possibilities down to the sixty-two included in this guide.

I have by no means found all the best places. As I proceeded with the project, I constantly discovered new places, either through someone's tip or just a reexamination of the maps. I'm sure there are still dozens of other lakes and ponds around New Hampshire and Vermont that really should be in a guide like this. That's what future editions are for. If anyone has suggestions of other lakes and ponds to add to this book, please pass them along to me: Alex Wilson, c/o AMC Books, 5 Joy Street, Boston, MA 02108. Also pass along any inaccuracies found in this edition, as well as suggestions for additional information that could be included in future editions.

Do I Really Want to Tell People about the Best Places?

Throughout this project, many people have asked me how I could tell others about my favorite hidden lakes and ponds—the remote, pristine places still unspoiled by too many people. After all, increased visitation would make these places less idyllic. That has indeed been a difficult issue for me and one I've spent many an hour grappling with as I paddled along.

What I've come to is this: by getting more people like you and me —people who value wild remote areas for what they are—out enjoying these places, we will be able to build support for greater protection of these bodies of water. For many lakes and ponds, protection means the purchase of fragile areas by such groups as the Nature Conservancy to prevent further development. On other bodies of water, the best form of protection is restriction on motorboat use, which is generally handled by state government. With some remote ponds, it is the surrounding land that needs protection and access restrictions. It is indeed a disappointment to spend half an hour carrying a canoe to a very remote pond only to find a bunch of oversized pickup trucks and other off-road vehicles chewing up the fragile wildflowers and driving in and out of the inlet streams.

My hope is that you will become involved in helping protect some of our most treasured water resources. For many of the lakes and ponds in New Hampshire and Vermont, the most vocal users right now are people who use motorboats to fish and water-ski. When surveys are done about the recreational use of these places, the loudest voice is from those people who are having the greatest impact on these delicate environments. The policy-makers need to hear from the low-impact users as well. I hope that in a few years I'll be able to report that many more of the lakes and ponds included here are better protected than they are today, and thus likely to remain enjoyable to quiet water paddlers for years and years to come.

Safety first

You might be attracted to quiet water because you paddle with small children and don't want to risk capsizing in a swift-flowing river. Or maybe you just don't like dangerous places such as raging white water on rivers in the spring, or places where you have to concentrate too much on your paddling skills. So you turn to the lakes and ponds, envisioning tranquil paddling on mirror-smooth water reflecting the surrounding mountains.

You will certainly find these places, including the idyllic mirror-smooth surfaces of mountain ponds at daybreak. But if you spend any time at all paddling around here, you will also encounter quite dangerous and even life-threatening conditions. Strong winds can come up very quickly in our mountains, turning that tranquil lake into a not-so-quiet white cap-filled inland sea. On a big lake, strong winds can stir up two-foot waves in almost no time—waves that are big enough to swamp a canoe. Unlike on rivers, on the larger lakes you are often far from shore, and capsizing in cold water can bring on hypothermia very quickly.

You may also need to beware of big boats with big wakes. On the narrow southern end of Lake Champlain, for example, large cabin cruisers heading for the New York Barge Canal can throw out a three-foot wake—more than enough to swamp a canoe. And there are horror stories of motorboat operators on big lakes such as Squam not even seeing canoes and colliding with them. A good motorboater will know to slow his or her boat when nearing paddlers, but you can't always count on that—believe me.

The bottom line is that you can encounter dangerous conditions on most lakes and ponds. You must always use care. Always bring proper life jackets, also known as personal floatation devices or PFDs (see further discussion of PFDs in the equipment section beginning on page xii). The best practice is to make it a rule to always wear your PFD in the canoe. Certainly all children should wear them, and if there are children in the boat, you too should wear a life jacket so that if the boat capsizes, you can be of more help to the children.

If you don't normally wear your life jacket while you paddle, at least put it on when wind comes up or when you're crossing a large lake. It may be an inconvenience, it may make you a little hotter in the summer, it may interfere a bit with your paddling. But it could save your life! So far, I've avoided any serious canoeing mishaps, but there have been numerous occasions—especially when my children were with me—when strong winds have come up unexpectedly, making me glad that we were well protected with high-quality life vests.

Also, in the name of safety, be ready to change your plans. If you've just driven four or five hours to get to one of the big, wild lakes

Be sure that children always wear properly fitting life vests in a canoe.

in northern New Hampshire and a gale is blowing, be ready to find a smaller pond that's more protected. I've made a point of including small ponds that are near some of the larger, better-known lakes for just this reason. Even if the forecaster promises a beautiful sunny day with no wind, it could end up blowing a gale and raining. So, be flexible in your plans.

On some lakes, ponds, and marshes described in this guide, you should also be aware that hunting season can bring a big influx of activity. I have tried to note those places where waterfowl hunting is popular—avoid these areas during hunting season. If you don't know when hunting season is, you can find out from state fish and wildlife officers. In New Hampshire, contact the New Hampshire Fish and Game Department, 2 Hazen Drive, Concord, NH 03301; 603-271-3212; in Vermont, contact the Vermont Fish and Wildlife Department, 103 South Main Street, Waterbury, VT 05676; 802-244-7331.

Starting Out Right: Equipment Selection

To get started with quiet water canoeing, you don't really need a whole lot of fancy, high-tech gear. Most any canoe will do, as long as it isn't a high-performance racing model or a tippy boat designed for white water. If you're new to canoeing, try to borrow a canoe for your first few trips. Once you've had a little experience, you'll be in a much better position to select a canoe to buy.

If you're buying a canoe, look for one that is stable. Canoe manufacturers often refer to both the initial stability and the secondary stability of their boats. A canoe with good initial stability and poor secondary stability will be unlikely to begin tipping, but once it tips up a bit it will probably keep going (this is the case with many older aluminum canoes). Look for a model that does well with both initial and secondary stability. The best canoe for lake and pond canoeing has a keel or shallow-V hull and straight keel-line to keep it tracking well across the water, even in a breeze. White-water canoes, on the other hand, have rounded bottoms and what's called *rocker,* or a curve to the bottom from front to back. Rocker provides manueverability in white water, but makes tracking very difficult on open water.

If you like the out-of-the-way lakes and ponds, especially those that require portaging in, you should try to stretch your budget to afford a Kevlar® canoe. Kevlar is a very strong fiber somewhat like fiberglass, but much lighter. My full-size Kevlar canoe weighs just fifty-five pounds, and my solo canoe (also Kevlar), around forty. If you plan to do a lot of canoeing by yourself, you should consider a solo canoe, in which you sit or kneel close to the center of the boat. You will be amazed at how easily a well-designed solo canoe handles compared with a standard two-seater used for solo canoeing.

Look for a good canoe carrying rack. I prefer a simple two-bar system that clips onto the car's rain gutters. You can save money by purchasing just the mounting brackets and cutting sections of two-by-four for the racks. (With newer cars that do not have gutters, you may need to buy one of the more expensive rack systems.) I strap the canoe to both racks and also secure it to both front and rear bumpers. The salespeople in any good outdoor equipment store should be able to set you up with an easy-to-use system.

Though not essential, a portage yoke in place of the center thwart makes portaging a lot easier (a thwart is a wood or metal support that spans the width of the canoe from gunwale to gunwale). If you expect to do a lot of portaging, you might also want a life vest with padded shoulders. Even with a portage yoke, this extra padding can make a long carry much more comfortable. Always attach a rope—called a painter—to the front of the canoe so that you can tie it up when you stop for lunch or, more important, so that the boat can be pulled if you get stuck or some other problem comes up.

Paddles should be light and comfortable. My favorite paddle is relatively short (fifty-six inches) with a blade made of various laminated woods, including both softwoods and hardwoods. It also has a special synthetic tip to protect the blade from damage if you hit rocks or push off from shore. You can try one of the new bent-shaft paddles, but I prefer a straight-shaft paddle.

As mentioned earlier, life preservers are a must—both by common sense and law. The best type of life preserver is a Coast Guard-approved Class I, II, or III personal floatation device or PFD. A Type IV PFD (floating cushion) is acceptable by law for adults, but far less effective than a life vest that you wear. A good life preserver is relatively expensive, but it is designed to keep a person's face above water even if he or she loses consciousness. There must be one PFD in the boat for each occupant, according to New Hampshire and Vermont laws. In Vermont, children twelve and under must wear a Type I, II, or III PFD. In New Hampshire, children six and under must wear a Type I, II, or III PFD. With children, it is extremely important that the PFD be the right size so that it won't slip off. Adult PFDs for children are not acceptable. If the adults in the canoe are not wearing their PFDs, they must be readily accessible. As described previously, however, I recommend that you wear your PFD at all times, especially if you're paddling with children.

As for clothing, plan for the unexpected—especially on long trips. Even with a bright sunny day forecast, I have frequently had a shower come along. So I make it a habit always to take a small stuff sack with my rain gear in the canoe. On longer trips I also carry a dry change of clothes. Along with rain coming up unexpectedly, temperatures can drop very quickly. Bring plenty of warm clothes if you will be out for a few hours with children. Be aware that they are probably just sitting while you are doing the work. Even though you may be plenty warm from the paddling, they can get cold. Watch for signs of discomfort.

Canoeing Technique

As with equipment selection, canoeing technique is a lot less critical with quiet water paddling than with white water canoeing, where it can literally mean the difference between life and death. On a quiet lake or pond it doesn't really matter whether you're using the proper J-stroke, or if you know the sweep stroke, the draw, or the reverse-J. Learning some of these strokes, however, can make a day of paddling more relaxing and enjoyable. I see lots of novices switching sides every few strokes—and even then the canoe weaves back and forth. It makes a lot more sense for the stern paddler to correct after each stroke or after every few strokes, so that it isn't necessary to switch sides all the time.

You can correct by using the paddle as a rudder at the end of the stroke, or by pushing out at the end of the stroke. If you use the same side of the blade to push out at the end of the stroke as you use for the power stroke, it's called a J-stroke (the thumb of the upper hand points *down* at the end of the stroke). If you pivot the paddle and push out with the face that was not used as the power stroke, you won't paddle quite as efficiently, but you won't tire as quickly either. Many canoe experts would scoff at the idea of using anything other than the proper J-stroke, but I don't think it makes much difference, as long as you can get where you want to go and can control the boat reasonably well. If you want to learn more about paddling strokes, consult one of the books on canoeing available at bookstores and libraries. Among the best books are *Beyond the Paddle* by Garret Conover (Tilbury House, 1991); *The Complete Wilderness Paddler* by Davidson and Rugge (Vintage, 1983), *The New Wilderness Canoeing and Camping* by Cliff Jacobson (ICS Books, 1986), and *Pole, Paddle & Portage* by Bill Riviere (Little, Brown & Co., 1969).

If you're a novice canoeist, I suggest starting out on the smaller lakes and ponds. Practice paddling into the wind, with the wind, and across it. Becoming comfortable with paddling isn't hard; it just takes some practice. On a warm day close to shore, you might even want to practice capsizing. That sounds odd, but intentionally tipping your canoe over will give you an idea of its limits and how easy or difficult it is to capsize. If you go that far with practicing, you might also try to get back into the canoe when you're away from shore. With two people, you should be able to right the boat by getting most of the water out (you'll need a bailer to get it all out). Then getting back in is a bit of a trick. Try it sometime—preferably *intentionally,* with an empty canoe near shore.

Bringing the Kids Along

Quiet water canoeing is a great activity to do with kids, as long as the conditions are all right and as long as you've made adequate provisions for safety. Maintain flexibility in your plans in case of adverse weather, and always make it a rule to wear life preservers in the canoe. We have a simple rule in our family: if you don't wear the vest, you don't get in the canoe. Period. To make wearing the vest more acceptable to our daughters (aged two and five), my wife and I also wear ours. Kids are more likely to don their vests if their parents do the same.

When paddling with kids you should also set up some rules about suddenly changing position in the boat. When both kids and the dog (well, that's another issue...) suddenly shift from one side of the canoe to the other, it can rock the boat precariously, especially if there's a strong breeze or waves. Two children side by side in the center of the canoe often works fairly well. We've rigged up a rope fence to keep our dog approximately in the center of the boat. Fortunately, we have a particularly mellow golden retriever, who is very good in a canoe; I wouldn't want to paddle with a lot of dogs I know.

My final suggestion for canoeing with kids—and perhaps the most important—is to make it fun. If the parents are arguing about who should be paddling on which side of the boat, or yelling about rocks ahead, the kids will be affected. Try to keep calm. Your kids will do better, and you'll have a better time. On long trips, such as across Squam Lake to a campsite or down the Magalloway River into Lake Umbagog, set up some cozy places where young children can sleep. We find that after the initial excitement of paddling fades, the gently rolling canoe puts our kids right to sleep, especially when we're returning from a several-day camping trip. If you haven't taken your kids canoeing before, they might be anxious on the first trip or two, but after they are used to it, they will be much more relaxed.

Canoe Camping

Canoe camping can provide a great way to spend a few days or even weeks in the outdoors. Usually you aren't too restricted as to what gear to bring, because, even with a couple of kids, a full-size canoe can hold a lot more gear than a couple of backpacks. You can bring pillows and a lantern along, and you don't have to carry your child in your arms when he or she decides enough is enough.

Canoe camping requires some careful planning, though. You not only have to get all the gear in the boat, but you need to get everything, including passengers, to balance properly so the canoe won't list to one side or sit lower in the water in the bow or the stern. How you plan depends on the type of trip it will be. If you will essentially be car camping with a canoe that you can park at the camp, that's one thing. Having to load all your gear into the canoe and head off for a few hours or more of paddling before setting up camp, takes much more careful planning.

With small children, especially kids in diapers, canoe camping can present special challenges—especially under adverse conditions, such as rain and approaching darkness while one adult is trying to set up the tent and the other is trying to get dinner ready before the kids fall apart. But if you plan carefully and reduce your expectations a little, canoe camping with kids is not that difficult. Of the twenty-plus nights we camped out with our two daughters this past season, there were just two or three really tense moments. Mostly this just takes practice, but there are some excellent books available to help you plan a canoe camping trip—including the excellent *Canoe Tripping with Children* by David and Judy Harrison (ICS Books, 1990).

Respect for the Outdoors

Lakes and ponds are among our most heavily used recreational areas. Keeping them in good shape requires special attention. Even a low-impact pastime such as canoeing or camping can have a substantial effect on a wilderness pond or remote lake-side campsite. Our wetlands are extremely important ecosystems for wildlife and home to many rare and endangered species. An unaware paddler can wreak havoc upon loons, otters, and fragile aquatic environments. Even too much paddling through a shallow marsh can injure the roots of ecologically important plants. So use care as you enjoy these waters. Special tips on how to observe wildlife with minimum impact are presented periodically throughout this guide.

The old adage "Take only photographs, leave only footprints" isn't enough for me. I make it a habit to carry a bag with me and pick up the leavings of less-thoughtful individuals who have used the lake or pond. If each of us can do the same, not only will we end up with much more attractive places to paddle, but we will also be appreciated. While motorboaters tend to have a bad reputation when it comes to leaving trash, I want canoeists to have the opposite reputation—which could come in handy when we are seeking greater paddling access on some of the region's more remote lakes. To learn more about how to enjoy a wild area without damaging it, see the excellent book *Soft Paths*, by Hampton and Cole (Stackpole Books, 1988).

What You'll See

Wetland ecosystems are diverse and exciting—by far the richest ecosystems we have access to. In New Hampshire and Vermont you can visit everything from salt-water estuarian marshes to deep crystal-clear alpine lakes and mysterious northern fens or bogs. You'll have the opportunity to observe hundreds of species of birds, dozens of species of mammals, turtles, snakes, and thousands of plants. Some of these species are quite rare and exciting to discover, such as the beautiful rose pogonia orchid, or a family of otters. But even ordinary plants and animals are a storehouse of information and discovery, providing hours of observation.

I've picked out a few of the more interesting animal species that you might encounter on the lakes and ponds of New Hampshire and Vermont and written up some notes on them. You will find these write-ups and accompanying pen-and-ink illustrations by Cathy Johnson interspersed in the lake and pond descriptions. By learning a little more about these species, you'll find them all the more fun to watch.

Have a Great Time

The purpose of this guide is to help you enjoy and appreciate our outdoors. I hope you will enjoy using this book as much as my family and I enjoyed researching and writing it. Let me know what you liked or disliked about the lakes and ponds I've included, and tell me about any others that you think should be included.

Finally, don't consider this guide as a limit to the areas you can visit. There are other lakes and ponds—hundreds more in our two states, many of which offer excellent quiet water canoeing. Buy some topographical or other maps and explore. You'll find, as I did, that some of the ponds shown on maps are municipal water supplies and off-limits to canoes. Others are inaccessible because of private land surrounding them. And others are too built up with summer homes. But there are many gems out there that are not written up in this guide— hidden beaver ponds, quiet meandering channels of slow-moving streams and rivers, old mill ponds with ruins of long-abandoned mills—places whose secrets you can either reveal to others or keep to yourself. And that's as it should be.

Alex Wilson
September 1991

How to Use This Book

For each lake or pond included in this book, a short descriptive write-up and map have been provided. Most maps show the roads or highways that provide access to the body of water, as well as boat launch sites. Some launch sites have boat ramps and are thus suitable for trailered motor boats as well as canoes, but many require a carry to the water. This latter type of launch site is not distinguished on the maps.

Note that many of the public boat access areas in Vermont are state fishing access sites. At one time, these launch sites could be used only by people engaged in fishing. The Vermont Department of Fish and Wildlife owns these sites, and most of the funding comes from hunting and fishing licenses. In recent years, however, federal funds became available to help support these access sites, and the restrictions on use have been relaxed. The current regulations state that the sites are to be used for fishing or for recreational gasoline-powered motorboat use as long as those uses do not interfere with fishing. Although recreational canoe use is not listed as a permitted use, I have been assured by the Department of Fish and Wildlife that canoeing is acceptable, although if parking is limited, priority is given to people who are fishing.

The maps and write-ups included in this guide are designed to accompany conventional road maps. If you are not familiar with your destination, do not try to rely on just these write-ups and maps to get there. At the very least, get a state highway map (they are available at most tourist information centers and interstate rest areas). Even better are more detailed maps, such as the excellent large-format New Hampshire and Vermont atlases published by DeLorme Mapping of Freeport, Maine. These atlases include small backcountry roads, some topographic features, and a wide assortment of useful information on hiking, state parks, private campgrounds, unusual natural features, fishing, and historical sites.

For additional information on fishing on these and other bodies of water, refer to DeLorme's *New Hampshire Fishing Maps* and Northern Cartographic's *Vermont Trout Ponds*. For more detailed information, buy the USGS topographical maps that cover the area. USGS maps are available in various scales. The most detailed are the 7$1/2$-minute and 7$1/2$ x 15-minute quadrangle maps. Depending on the maps, the scale of them is either 1:24,000 or 1:25,000 (metric). Most of the 7$1/2$-minute and 7$1/2$ x 15-minute maps for Vermont and New Hampshire were updated in the 1980s, so they are relatively current.

If you're interested in something more sophisticated than camping, check your local bookstore or library for guides to bed-and-breakfasts or country inns, many of which can be found near the lakes and ponds in this guide. You might also want to contact Chambers of Commerce to get more information on lodging, restaurants, and area attractions.

Several different terms are used throughout this book to identify a body of water—primarily lake, pond, and reservoir. Though there are some differences in these terms (a lake is usually bigger than a pond, and reservoirs are always manmade), they are often used interchangeably. I have tried to stick with the term most widely used in referring to each body of water, but confusion can arise. As for distinguishing between natural and artificial bodies of water, I have made little attempt to do so. The vast majority of lakes and ponds in the two states have dams and are thus "artificial" to some extent, though most existed before damming; the dam simply raised the water level.

Finally, while the book is about quiet water canoeing, the information applies equally well to kayaking. Many of the lakes and ponds included would also be fine for sculling, though others do not have suitable access.

Key to Maps in Text

⌒	Tent site	
◀	Lean-to	
⊼	Picnic area	
Ⲗ	State or federal campground	
◬	Private campground	
⌣	Boat access	
P	Parking area	
	Marsh	
	Peak	
	Interstate highway	═══════
	State highway	▬▬▬▬▬
	Paved road	▬•▬•▬•▬
	Graded dirt road	══════
	Rough dirt road	= = = = = =
	Foot path	··············
	River	══⟶══
	Stream	──⟶──

arrow indicates direction of flow

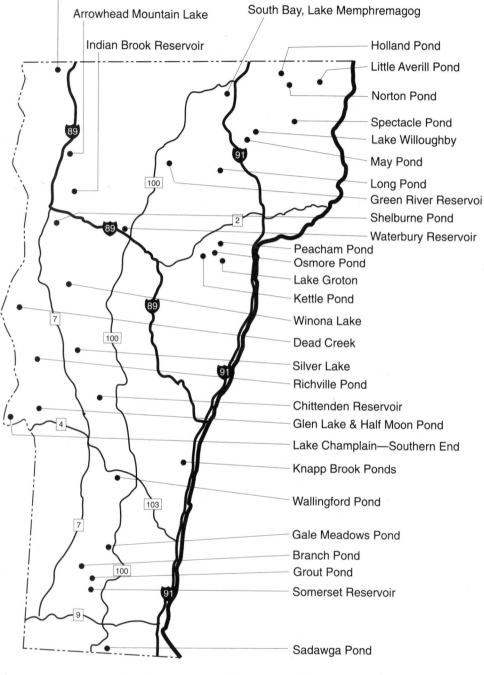

Missisquoi Delta, Lake Champlain

Arrowhead Mountain Lake

Indian Brook Reservoir

South Bay, Lake Memphremagog

Holland Pond

Little Averill Pond

Norton Pond

Spectacle Pond

Lake Willoughby

May Pond

Long Pond

Green River Reservoi

Shelburne Pond

Waterbury Reservoir

Peacham Pond

Osmore Pond

Lake Groton

Kettle Pond

Winona Lake

Dead Creek

Silver Lake

Richville Pond

Chittenden Reservoir

Glen Lake & Half Moon Pond

Lake Champlain—Southern End

Knapp Brook Ponds

Wallingford Pond

Gale Meadows Pond

Branch Pond

Grout Pond

Somerset Reservoir

Sadawga Pond

Lakes and Ponds: Vermont

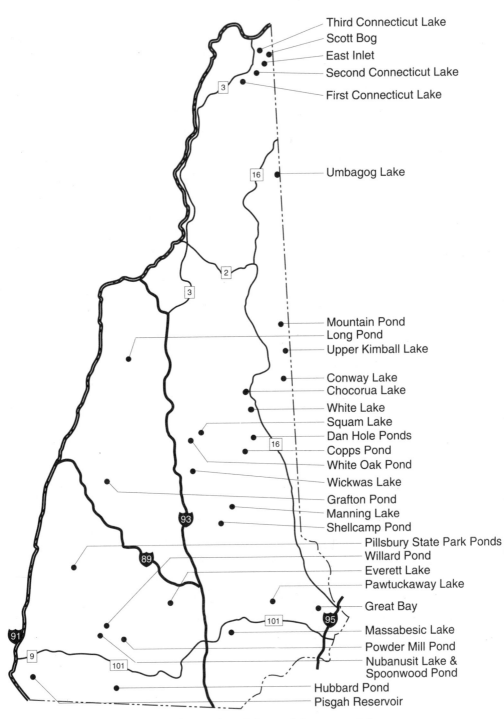

Third Connecticut Lake
Scott Bog
East Inlet
Second Connecticut Lake
First Connecticut Lake

Umbagog Lake

Mountain Pond
Long Pond
Upper Kimball Lake

Conway Lake
Chocorua Lake

White Lake
Squam Lake
Dan Hole Ponds
Copps Pond
White Oak Pond

Wickwas Lake

Grafton Pond
Manning Lake
Shellcamp Pond

Pillsbury State Park Ponds
Willard Pond
Everett Lake
Pawtuckaway Lake

Great Bay

Massabesic Lake
Powder Mill Pond
Nubanusit Lake &
Spoonwood Pond

Hubbard Pond
Pisgah Reservoir

Lakes and Ponds: New Hampshire

Southern
New Hampshire

Pisgah Reservoir
Winchester, NH

Despite its proximity to quite populated areas, Pisgah Reservoir, in the southwestern corner of New Hampshire, is one of the most remote bodies of water included in this book. It is hidden deep in the hills of Pisgah State Park. To get there you have to drive on Reservoir Road, an unimproved dirt road, for a mile and a half. Drive carefully, especially if your vehicle has low ground clearance, like my VW Rabbit. At the end of Reservoir Road you still have a steep half-mile carry with switchbacks into the reservoir. With a light solo canoe (about forty pounds), the hike in took me about twenty minutes. If you have a heavy canoe, or one without a good portage yoke, plan on lots of rests on the steep carry. (When you get to the very steep switchback, you're almost there.) At the trail intersection, turn left to get to the dam for launching, or simply head through the woods to the lake, which you'll see from there. All the hard work is worth it!

The small (110-acre) but highly varied reservoir is gorgeous, with many islands, deep inlets, and hidden coves. Total length from one end to the other is about a mile and a half, but the reservoir offers over five miles of shoreline to explore. The water is quite deep and exceptionally clean, with no motorboats, houses, or summer camps to spoil it. The surrounding shoreline is heavily wooded; hemlock and white pine are the dominant species, interspersed with various hardwoods, including red oak, beech, red maple, and birch (both yellow and white). At water's edge the banks are thick with blueberry bushes in some areas. Most of the shoreline is rocky, with some marshy areas in the longer inlets, where you are likely to see an occasional pair of nesting ducks. At the extreme northern end and in some of the shallow inlets, pond

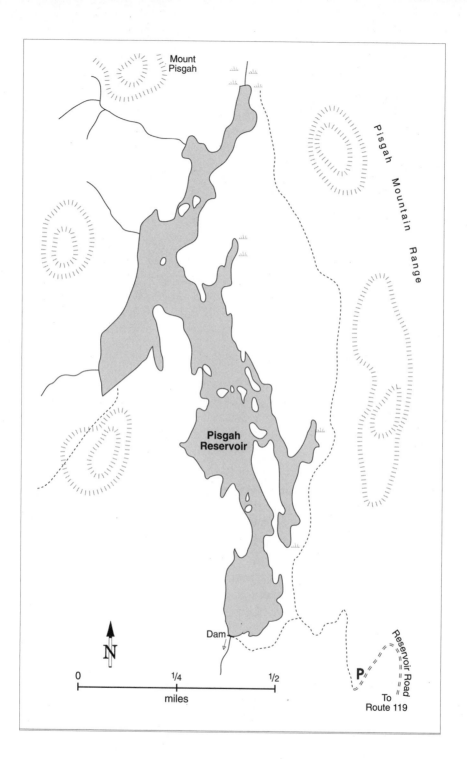

Mount Pisgah

Pisgah Mountain Range

Pisgah Reservoir

Dam

N

0   1/4   1/2

miles

P

Reservoir Road

To
Route 119

Because you have to carry your canoe into Pisgah Reservoir, you're unlikely to see many other paddlers here.

At the extreme northern end and in some of the shallow inlets, pond vegetation can be fairly thick, but most of the lake is open.

Besides the main reservoir, Pisgah State Park has a number of smaller ponds including Fullam, Lily, Baker, Tufts, and Kilburn. Most of these other ponds are in the northern half of the park and reachable via hiking trails or unimproved dirt roads. There are access points to Pisgah State Park on all sides, and a half-dozen parking areas at trailheads. Pick up a trail map in the mailbox at the bottom of Reservoir Road, or at one of the other access points to the park. Camping and fires are not permitted in the park, so you are limited to day trips only. Hunting is permitted so you may want to schedule trips when hunting season is not open.

GETTING THERE: Reservoir Road can be reached from Route 119, 2.4 miles east of the turnoff for Route 63 North in Hinsdale. The gate is open daily from the end of mud season (May 23 is the date given, but it can vary considerably) until snow makes passage difficult (usually November or December). In the morning the gate is opened by 9:00, and it is usually closed around dusk. During the week the gate is sometimes left open all night, enabling you to get a much earlier start in the morning (when you're more likely to see wildlife). For more information and a trail map, call Pisgah State Park at 603-239-8153, or write to Pisgah State Park, P.O. Box 242, Winchester, NH 03470.

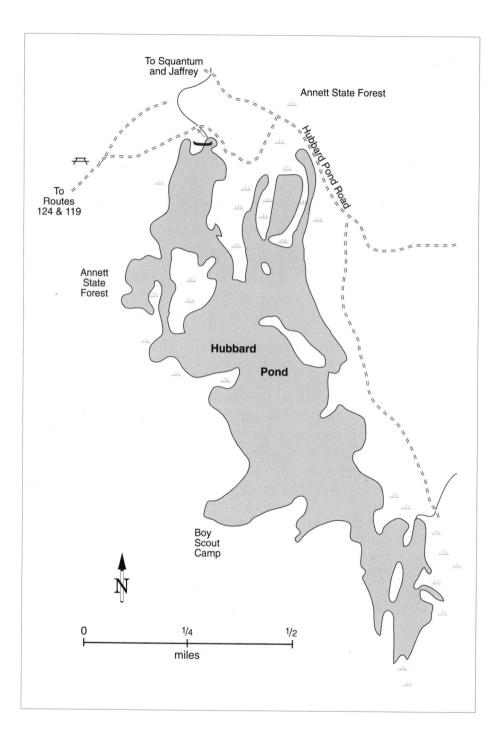

Hubbard Pond

Rindge, NH

Hubbard Pond is one of those hidden treasures in southern New Hampshire. Even most of the people living nearby don't know about it. Except for a Boy Scout camp on the southern end used June through August, Hubbard is totally undeveloped. Limited and unmarked access via an unimproved dirt road through Annett State Forest should ensure that the lake remains relatively unspoiled. Hubbard Pond seems a lot larger than it is (about 250 acres) because of the many marshy inlets and islands. Most of the lake is shallow and parts of it are quite choked with weeds, which makes it a great spot for painted turtles, ducks, wading birds, beavers and even the occasional otter. By midsummer, however, vegetation can make the going pretty difficult on the shallowest parts of the lake.

Despite the marshiness along much of the shore, the ground rises quickly on the eastern shore and most islands, so you can get up on solid ground for a picnic lunch. Up on the high banks you'll see plenty of evidence of beavers cutting hemlock saplings.

The best time for visiting Hubbard Pond is in the spring or fall, when the Boy Scout camp is not operating, though you might also want to visit in midsummer, when the prolific high-bush blueberries will be ripe. With a view of Mount Monadnock to the northwest, this is a great lake for enjoying the autumn foliage. Though the lake is fairly well protected, high winds can blow out of the nearby hills, making canoeing difficult at times. Keep close to shore when it's windy.

GETTING THERE: You can drive into the northern end of Hubbard Pond and park by a small concrete dam, either on a dead-end dirt road accessible from Cathedral Road or from Hubbard Pond Road. Driving from the west on Route 119, turn left onto Cathedral Road, approximately 1.2 miles east of Route 202. Drive northeast on Cathedral Road for roughly 2.4 miles, and then turn right onto an unimproved road into Annett State Forest and to Hubbard Pond. Be careful in the early spring or after rain—these unimproved roads can be difficult to travel. In mid-April, just after ice-out, I was glad to have four-wheel drive!

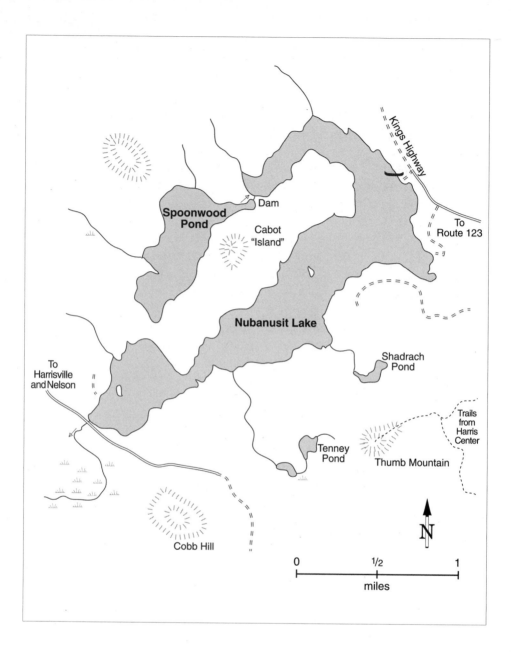

Nubanusit Lake and Spoonwood Pond
Hancock, NH

Nubanusit Lake would be one of southern New Hampshire's real gems if motorboating were more restricted. On a summer weekend, the speedboats and water-skiers can be oppressive on the 640-acre lake, and even dangerous. Fortunately for canoeists, there is a solution: paddle northwest from the boat launch (keeping to the shore, where the larger motorboats will keep their distance) and then around the bend to the southwest. At the dam, carry your boat over to the outlet of Spoonwood Pond, and you're free at last. The water level of Spoonwood was about four feet lower than it should have been when I visited, as water had undermined Spoonwood Dam. This made the channel into Spoonwood quite narrow and the current fairly noticeable. At this writing the status of dam repairs was not known.

Spoonwood Pond is a well-protected pond unaccessible by car and off-limits to motorboats. Like Nubanusit, the 144-acre Spoonwood has a rocky shoreline, and in some places giant slabs of granite extend down to and under the water line. For the geologist, this is an interesting spot. Very large feldspar crystals can be found in the granite (making it look almost like a conglomerate rock), as well as mica, garnets, and iron deposits. From Spoonwood Pond you can hike through heavily wooded rocky terrain on Cabot "Island" (not really an island), owned by Keene State College, crossing to the southern end of Nubanusit Lake if you want to watch motorboats, or you can stick to the eastern side of the lake and hike on wilderness land owned or managed by the Harris Center.

Both Nubanusit and Spoonwood have exceptionally clean water, and both have excellent reputations for cold-water fish, including salmon and trout (lake, brook, and rainbow). You can also catch pickerel and yellow perch.

Camping is not permitted here, though there are a couple of state parks with camping within a relatively short drive: Greenfield State Park (603-547-3497) and Monadnock State Park (603-532-8862). Refer to the New Hampshire State Highway Map or the *New Hampshire Atlas and Gazetteer* (DeLorme Mapping) for the location of these and area private campgrounds.

GETTING THERE: To reach the boat landing at Nubanusit Lake, drive southeast on Route 123 from Route 9 in South Stoddard. After 4.7 miles, make a sharp right turn. Go another 0.4 mile and turn right onto Kings Highway, which isn't much of a highway at all (a sign to the Harris Center points to the left here). The boat access is on the left, 1.1 miles down Kings Highway. There is very little parking room here, and on a busy weekend day you may not find room to park—another reason why it's better to visit midweek or before Memorial Day or after Labor Day. If it's too crowded, visit some of the other bodies of water in the area (see sections on Willard Pond and Powder Mill Pond).

During a day's outing, you might want to visit the Harris Center for Conservation Education, a few minutes down King's Highway (a dirt road) from the landing at Nubanusit Lake. The Harris Center includes a network of hiking trails and a wonderful old estate where it holds educational programs. A trail from the Harris Center leads to Thumb Mountain, which overlooks Tenney Pond and Shadrach Pond. For information contact The Harris Center, King's Highway, Hancock, NH 03449; 603-525-3394.

Willard Pond

Antrim, NH

Hidden in the southwestern part of New Hampshire, protected by an Audubon Society preserve, lies Willard Pond. This small (100 acre) pond is simply breathtaking. Moss-covered granite boulders dot the shoreline, which is wooded with mountain laurel, yellow birch, beech, red oak, red maple, and white pine. The water is crystal clear, letting you see down at least fifteen feet. The clarity of the water is actually disconcerting, because at first glance a boulder two feet underwater looks as if it's almost breaking the water—then you glide right over it.

Nearly the entire surrounding area is a wildlife preserve owned and managed by the New Hampshire Audubon Society. For the bird-watcher there are two trails around a good part of the lake and plenty of opportunity to observe birds from a canoe. The shore is alive with the singing of warblers, sparrows, and a wide assortment of other song-birds. You may also hear the enchanting wail of the lake's nesting loon pair (be very careful not to disturb nesting loons—see page 51). Several marshy inlets provide ideal habitat for ducks and herons. The property is obviously well managed; in fact, I had a lot of trouble finding a piece of trash to take with me (a little compulsion I've developed is

Though small, Willard Pond is one of the most pristine bodies of water in southern New Hampshire—perfect for a quiet morning or afternoon of solo paddling.

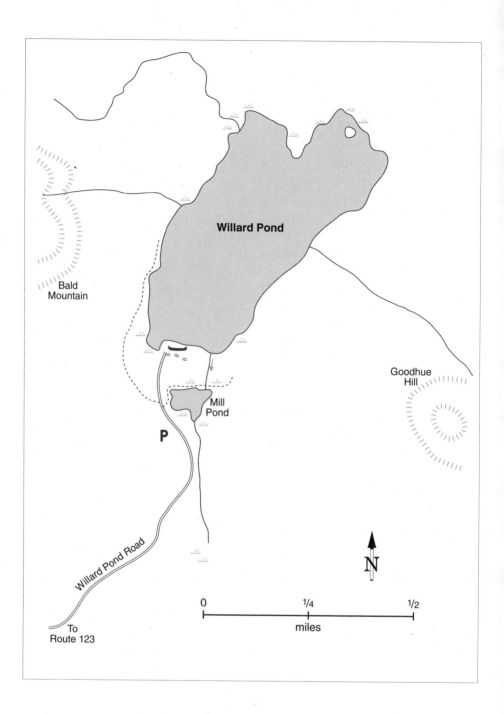

Willard Pond

Bald
Mountain

Goodhue
Hill

Mill
Pond

P

Willard Pond Road

To
Route 123

N

0   1/4   1/2
miles

piece of trash to take with me (a little compulsion I've developed is always to collect some litter that others have left).

GETTING THERE: Coming from the south or east, take Route 123 northwest from Hancock, approximately three miles from the intersection of Routes 123 and 137. Turn right onto an unmarked dirt road. The pond is approximately 1.5 miles down this road. Coming from the north or west, go southeast on Route 123, 3.2 miles from the intersection with Route 9 in Stoddard. Turn left onto an unmarked dirt road (Willard Pond Road), which feeds into the other access road off Route 123 after 0.5 miles. You can drive right to the water to unload your canoe, but you must drive back and park your vehicle at the large parking lot. Gasoline-powered motorboats are prohibited from Willard Pond, and the fishing is restricted to fly fishing. There is one privately owned house at the southern end of the pond, but the house is set back from the water and hardly visible from the pond. For more information on Willard Pond, contact the Audubon Society of New Hampshire, P.O. Box 528-B, Concord, NH 03302; 603-224-9909.

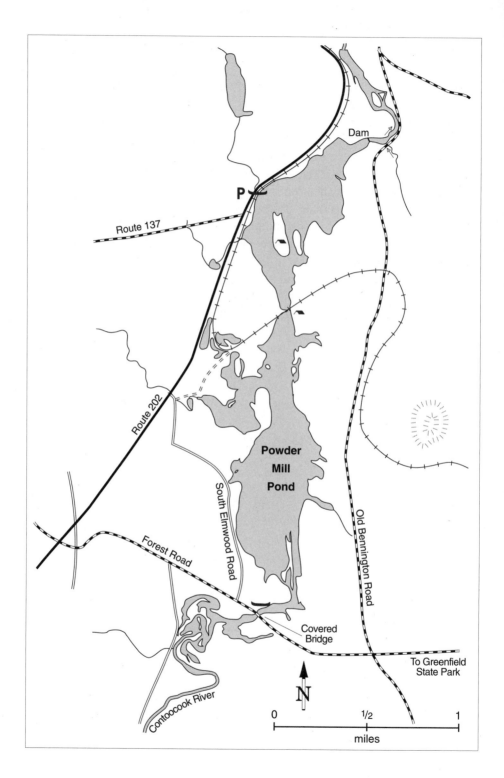

Dam

P

Route 137

Route 202

Powder
Mill
Pond

South Elmwood Road

Old Bennington Road

Forest Road

Covered
Bridge

To Greenfield
State Park

Contoocook River

N

0   1/2   1
miles

Powder Mill Pond
Hancock and Greenfield, NH

The Contoocook River is dammed up in Bennington, New Hampshire, to form Powder Mill Pond, an unspoiled pond of about 350 acres. Development is limited to a few old farms along the western shore. The primary drawback is road noise from Route 202, which runs quite close to the pond at the northern end. Because Powder Mill Pond is a public water supply, gasoline-powered motorboats are prohibited, though people who are fishing may use electric motors. You'll find lots of deep inlets and marshy eddies to explore along the nearly three-mile stretch from the covered bridge on Forest Road at the southern end of the pond to the dam at the northern end. The water is exceptionally clean, as evidenced by the shells of freshwater mussels along the shore—left by raccoons, probably.

Close to the northern end of the lake are two islands with six or seven unmaintained group campsites that are accessible by canoe. (I was told by an unofficial source that camping is permitted here, but have not been able to verify it.) Another campsite can be found on the eastern side of the lake just south of the railroad trestle (which you practically have to duck under to pass through). The island campsites are fairly obvious from the water; the site on the eastern shore may require more scouting. Family camping is available nearby at Greenfield State Park P.O. Box 203, Greenfield, NH; 603-547-3497. Drive east on Forest Road about three miles from the covered bridge to get there.

GETTING THERE: To get to Powder Mill Pond, take Route 202 north from Peterborough. To reach the southern access point, continue on Route 202 about one mile north of the turnoff for Route 123 West and turn right onto Forest Road. Take Forest Road 1.2 miles to the covered bridge, where you can pull over and carry a canoe down to the water. To put in near the northern end of the pond, continue north on Route 202. Just past the turnoff for Route 137 West, Route 202 comes quite close to the pond. There is parking for several cars on the east side of the road along here, but the best parking area—especially for overnight parking—is across the road (on the west side) just north of the most obvious put-in spot.

From detailed topographic maps, it looks as if the area just upstream (south) from the covered bridge would also be very nice for canoeing, though I have not yet paddled here. This section of the Contoocook River twists and folds tightly, leaving many islands and oxbow curves to explore.

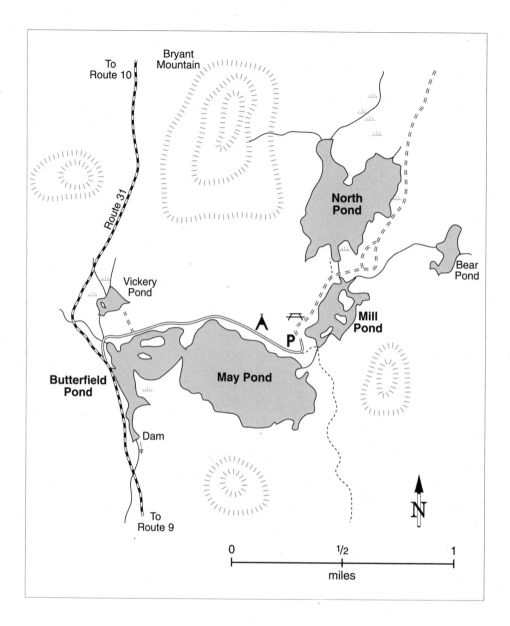

Pillsbury State Park Ponds:
Butterfield, May, Mill, and North Ponds

Washington, NH

The string of four small ponds in Pillsbury State Park, which are the headwaters of the Aschuelot River, offer superb quiet water canoeing, particularly if an overnight is desired. Butterfield, the farthest downstream, extends from a dam next to Route 31. A narrow, rocky strait connects Butterfield to May Pond, the largest and deepest of the lakes. I saw loons on both May and Butterfield and believe two pairs may have been resident in 1991.

There are a dozen or so camping sites along the northern shore of May Pond, some beautifully situated on the water. These sites are open year-round and are free off-season when the park office is closed. In season, you will pay a reasonable $10 to $12 per site per night (1990 rates). For information, contact Pillsbury State Park, Washington, NH, 03280; 603-863-2860.

Near the eastern end of May Pond, you can portage along an open trail and road up to Mill Pond, or you can drive; there is parking for about 15 cars. Mill Pond is quite small and shallow. Much of the surface is covered with pond weeds during the summer months, making paddling difficult. But you're likely to see more wildlife here, such as the pair of hooded mergansers I watched feeding in late April.

The adventurous can take out at the inlet into Mill Pond and portage up to North Pond, the most remote of the four ponds. Take out on the right side of the inlet (facing upstream) and carry a few dozen yards to the woods road. Take the road to the left (back toward the parking area at Mill Pond), cross the bridge, and then take the trail to the right after fifty or sixty yards. This trail leads a few hundred yards to North Pond. You can also portage up from Mill Pond, but the carry is a lot longer. (The road is not maintained past Mill Pond, and driving is not recommended.)

North Pond has the feel of northern Canadian wilderness. It is a rich, marshy fen, with birds galore and one of the most curious of plant species: the northern pitcher plant. Look for these insect-eating reddish plants on the numerous low islands, sphagnum moss hummocks, or shoreline amid the dense creeping cranberry bushes and other heaths. Like Mill Pond, North Pond is fairly thick with vegetation during the summer months, but that shouldn't stop you from enjoying this bit of the wilderness.

North Pond is the most remote of the four ponds in Pillsbury State Park. There's a nice picnic area along the northeastern shore.

The surrounding woodlands are generally deciduous, with red maple, yellow birch, beech, and other species, though there is enough fir and pine to provide contrast. When you tire of paddling, you can enjoy some of the wonderful trails around these ponds and through the hills, including hikes into the smaller Vickery and Bear Ponds. Pick up a map at the park office just as you turn into the park from Route 31.

GETTING THERE: To reach Pillsbury State Park from the east, take Route 31 northwest from Route 9 near Hillsboro. The park entrance is on the right about 13.5 miles from Route 9. From the north coming down Route 10, turn onto Route 31 South just past Goshen. The park entrance is on the left in about 4.7 miles. Coming from the south or west, take Route 10 North to the turn off for Route 31 South. The entrance to the park is well marked.

The Spectacular Wood Duck
Colorful Dweller of the Wetlands

CATHY JOHNSON

If you have yet to see a male wood duck, you're in for a treat on your paddling trips. Of all our ducks—perhaps of all our bird species—nothing approaches a wood duck in sheer beauty. With distinctive multicolored breeding plumage, iridescent in the sunlight, the male wood duck is something to behold. Getting a good look at wood ducks, though, requires some quiet paddling, for they are extremely wary. Look for them in marshy areas as you paddle around grassy islands and meandering inlet channels.

Most of the time, the only glimpse you'll get of wood ducks is as they fly away.

The wood duck, *Aix sponsa*, is unusual for several other reasons, most notably its nesting habits. Unlike most ducks, wood ducks nest in trees, in abandoned woodpecker holes, cavities hollowed out by decay, and, more recently, artificial nesting boxes. Sharp down-curving claws on the toes help the birds cling to tree trunks. They can also walk or run overland far better than most other ducks. I remember being quite surprised when canoeing on Umbagog Lake to see a female wood duck with a string of chicks swim to the shore and then run into the protective vegetation—it seemed so unducklike! When danger threatens, wood ducks can dive and even swim underwater for a fair distance.

Wood ducks pair up in the fall or winter in the Southeast, where New England's wood ducks overwinter. The pair migrates north, with the male following the female to the area—usually the same pond—where she was raised. In very early spring the female selects a suitable nesting cavity, which may be from four to fifty feet up in a tree and over water or land.

The hen lays ten to fifteen eggs in very early spring. When the young hatch, all within a few hours of each other, they stay in the nest for only a day. Then, after carefully checking for signs of danger, the mother flies down to the water or ground below and calls to the chicks. Without hesitation, they jump out of the nest, using the sharp claws on their toes to climb up to the opening. Short stubby wings and downy feathers slow the chicks' descent, and remarkably, even when jumping from a nest fifty feet above ground, they seldom get hurt. They may bounce on the ground and be stunned for a moment, but a few seconds later, they are up and clustering around their mother.

The chicks can swim right away, but sometimes they must walk up to a mile overland to reach water. This is the most perilous time for the young, and many are lost to predators such as mink and fox before reaching water. In the water they may be prey to large fish (bass, northern pike, pickerel) and snapping turtles. The chicks grow quickly during the summer and can fly by the time they are eight to ten weeks old.

The male wood duck molts during the summer, losing his beautiful breeding plumage until fall. In the nonbreeding, or eclipse, plumage, the male is harder to distinguish from the female (if you get a close look, the male retains his red eyes and bill, and the female has distinct white eye rings). For a two- to three-week period during molting, the male cannot fly. The female also goes through a molt a little later than the male, but her plumage does not change significantly in appearance.

In the fall, wood ducks congregate in larger numbers, especially in the evening. Sometimes hundreds or even thousands of wood ducks fly to the same roosting pond each evening and leave at daybreak to feed on nearby ponds and streams. By mid-fall, most of New England's wood ducks have left to migrate south. They usually travel in small, loosely aggregated flocks.

While wood duck populations are relatively strong today, the species was hunted almost to extinction around the turn of the century. Protective legislation was passed after the U.S. Biological Survey reported in 1901 that wood ducks faced possible extinction. At this time the newly formed National Audubon Society and a few other organizations began a long, slow effort to get federal legislation enacted.

The Weeks-McLean Act, the first national legislation protecting waterfowl, was passed in 1913, and even greater protection was won by the Migratory Bird Treaty Act, which was signed into law in 1918. This treaty extended protection of wood ducks and other migrating birds to Canada, gave the federal government greater authority to regulate hunting, and prohibited the sale of wildfowl. The hunting season on wood ducks was completely closed by the United States and Canada until 1941, when the species had recovered enough to allow a limited fall season.

The recovery of wood ducks in the Northeast was set back by the 1938 hurricane, which blew down many old trees that had provided nesting cavities. To provide more sites, the first artificial nesting boxes were put up in Great Meadows National Wildlife Refuge near Concord, Massachusetts, and the idea soon spread around the country. Today, thousands of wood duck nesting boxes are used throughout the East. You are likely to see these boxes as you paddle around the ponds, lakes, and marshes in New Hampshire and Vermont. Metal cones beneath the boxes or metal flashing around the post holding the box keep predators away, especially raccoons and snakes.

The biggest threat to wood ducks today is loss of suitable nesting habitat. Wood ducks need remote ponds and marshes to raise their young, and these areas are increasingly threatened by encroaching development.

Everett Lake
Weare, NH

Created in 1962 by an Army Corps of Engineers flood-control dam on the Piscataquog River in Weare, New Hampshire, Everett Lake offers pleasant canoeing, picnicking, and swimming. Motorboats are prohibited from the 150-acre lake, and there is no development other than the dam and recreational facilities. Paddling around the lake, there is no mistaking that it is an artificial body of water, especially with the large 250-foot high dam looming over much of the lake. But if you paddle toward the northern end, through the winding, marshy channels full of pickerelweed and waterlilies, it looks and feels much more natural.

GETTING THERE: The best way into the lake is through Clough State Park. If you're driving from the Manchester area, take Route 114 North. Check your odometer when Route 13 North splits off at Goffstown, and continue another 2.8 miles. Then turn right onto New Boston Road East. Almost immediately turn right onto Riverdale Road, and then left onto River Road. Drive north on River Road for 2.6 miles and take a right onto Clough Park Road. The park entrance is 2.1 miles up this road on the left.

Unfortunately, Clough State Park is not always open. From Memorial Day until late June, the park is open only during weekends. From late June until Labor Day, it is open daily. When in use, the gates open at 9:00 A.M. and close at 7:30 P.M. In 1991, rates were $2.50 per person per day, with children twelve and under free.

You can still get onto the lake when the park is closed, however, by continuing past it (passing Alexander Road to the left) for 1.9 miles and bearing left onto Mansion Road. In just over a half-mile, Mansion Road curves sharply to the right; continue straight on a poorly maintained road marked: "HOP-EV Parking." This road leads into a road and trail network for off-road vehicles. Continue on the main road south toward the lake for 1.5 miles. A fork to the left leads into one arm of the lake, but there may be a gate here. If you turn right instead, you will cross over a small inlet to the lake in another 0.2 mile. You can pull over by the little bridge and carry your canoe down to the water (on the left side of the road). A short paddle past a beaver lodge leads into the main lake. This road winds around the reservoir and leads back to River Road in 2.6 miles. This access isn't as convenient as Clough Park, but with the park closed, there will be far fewer people on the lake, which compensates for the effort.

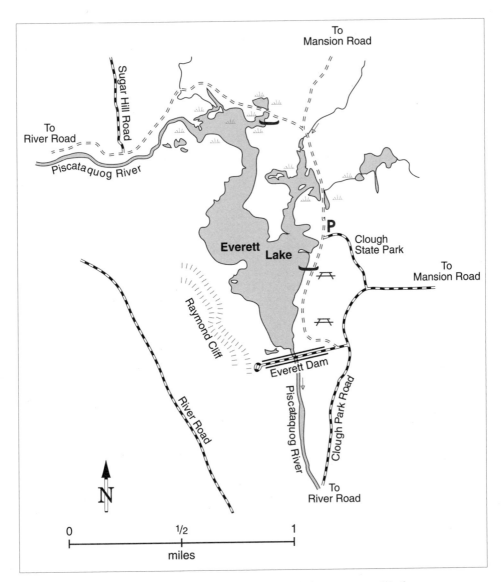

To Mansion Road

To River Road

Sugar Hill Road

Piscataquog River

Everett Lake

P

Clough State Park

To Mansion Road

Raymond Cliff

River Road

Everett Dam

Piscataquog River

Clough Park Road

To River Road

N

0   1/2   1
miles

On the marshy northeastern end of the lake, you are likely to see great blue herons, painted turtles, and various ducks. On the larger, more western arm of the lake extending north, you reach a sandy-bottomed inlet creek lined with alders and willows, but this creek is too shallow to paddle more than a few hundred feet. Most of the lake shoreline is open and sandy with white pines on the higher land. You'll find picnic tables at various open locations around the lake. Watch out for poison ivy, though—I saw lots of it here. For more information on the park, contact Clough State Park, 120 East Dunbarton Road, Goffstown, NH 03045; 603-529-7112. There is no camping in the park.

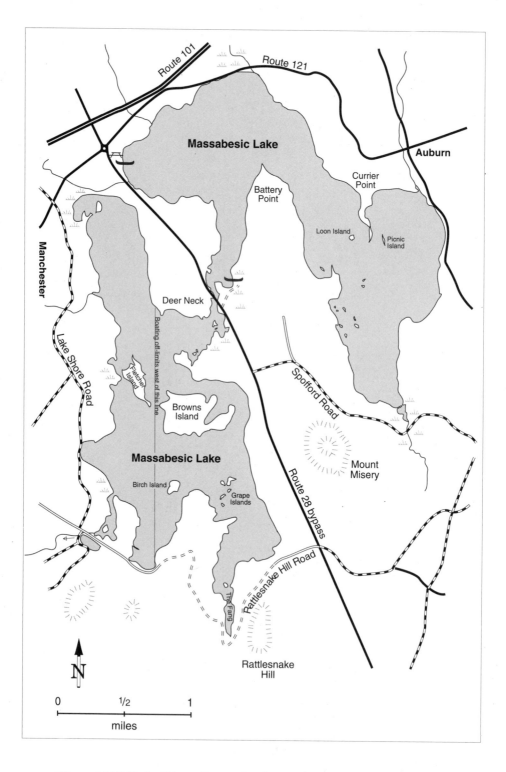

Massabesic Lake
Manchester and Auburn, NH

Massabesic Lake serves as the water supply for the city of Manchester, so, there are restrictions on how the lake may be used. Specifically, there is no swimming or water-skiing, and a portion of the 2,500-acre lake is off-limits to all boating. Despite this—and in part because of it—Massabesic offers superb canoeing. The water is extremely clean and crystal clear. There is almost no development along the shore, and the houses that are there somehow seem less intrusive because swimming is prohibited. Indeed, it is a real surprise to find such a large and relatively pristine lake so close to New Hampshire's largest city.

Because of its smaller size and greater shoreline variation, the lower section of the lake is a little nicer for canoeing. The western half of this section of the lake is off-limits to boating of any kind. You will see a line of buoys that divide the lake in half along the Manchester city line, with clearly marked signs indicating the restriction.

The shoreline is generally rocky by the water, then heavily wooded further inland. The dominant trees are white pine, red pine, red maple, white birch, and red oak, but you will also see some black gum growing along the water's edge. Black gum is one of the first trees to turn red in the fall, and its brilliant foliage is stunning. I've also seen a few surviving American chestnut trees here. If you visit in midsummer, you'll find lots of high-bush blueberries. Also keep an eye out for loons, which often nest here (but be careful not to disturb them; see page 51).

The Grape Islands near the southern end are definitely worth a visit, and you might want to paddle into the deep cove called the Fang at the southern tip. Near the inlet from the upper section of Massabesic Lake, close to the road, there is a small marshy area that is usually canoeable. You're likely to see great blue herons, wood ducks, and assorted other water birds here, and possibly beaver. Massabesic is best-known for its smallmouth bass and pickerel, but brown trout, horned pout, yellow perch, and white perch are also caught here.

The upper portion of the lake can also be nice, though it is larger, with bigger motorboats and sailboats. On a breezy day or a sunny summer weekend, you'll do much better to stick to the lower section of the lake.

Despite its close proximity to New Hampshire's largest city, Massabesic Lake offers superb canoeing.

GETTING THERE: The boat access for the southern section of Massabesic Lake is just off the Route 28 bypass, 1.7 miles south of Route 101 (Exit 1). Driving south, you will see the pull-off on the left, just after crossing the bridge over the channel that connects the two sections of the lake. If you want to canoe on the upper portion, there is a large park and picnic area on the east side of the Route 28 bypass, just south of the circle where Route 121 intersects, where you can put a boat in. The boat ramp is on the northern section of the lake, but it takes just a few minutes to paddle south, under the bridge, to get into the quieter southern section.

Pawtuckaway Lake

Nottingham, NH

Pawtuckaway Lake is a large (903 acre) body of water well known for its bass fishing. The shoreline is highly varied with numerous coves, inlets, and islands. Unfortunately, the eastern shore and the southern end are heavily developed. For canoeing, the best area is the northern end, especially Fundy Cove, which extends to the west. There is no development in this cove and almost none around the northern end down to Log Cabin Island. South of the island, the eastern shore and its numerous coves are dotted with both seasonal and year-round houses.

GETTING THERE: The put-in point for the northern end is off Deerfield Road, which extends around the northern end of the lake. Stay on Deerfield Road 2.0 miles past the intersection with Route 156, and turn left onto an unmarked dirt road. Follow this road 0.5 mile to the boat access, where you will find plenty of parking on all but the busiest weekends. The access is located within Pawtuckaway State Park, which bounds most of the western side of the lake.

Several islands and a highly varied shoreline offer plenty of opportunity for exploration in the northern end of Pawtuckaway Lake.

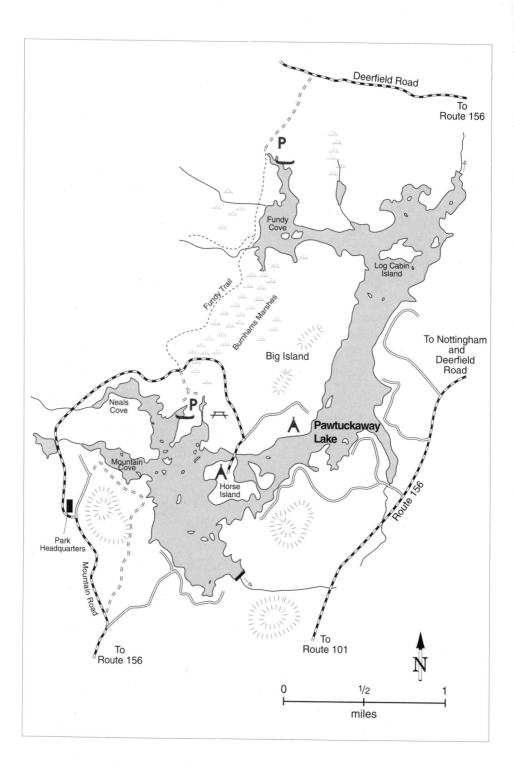

From the boat access you can paddle south into Fundy Cove and then east into the main lake. The shoreline is heavily wooded, with white pine, red maple, white birch, and hemlock the dominant species. The understory is generally quite open, providing easy access onto the shore for a picnic lunch or a rest. In mid- to late summer, your progress may be slowed by a profusion of high-bush blueberries growing along the shores. Most of the inlets are quite marshy, offering good birding habitat.

Paddling on the lake, be careful of large rocks at or just below the surface. Paddling with my dog, I managed to hang myself up on a somewhat concave boulder that lurked an inch or two beneath the surface of the water, and I had quite a time getting off it (fortunately, my dog was patient). At the northeast tip of the lake, there is a nice beach owned by the town of Nottingham (swimming here is limited to Nottingham residents, and boats are not permitted in the beach area). Nearby is the north outlet dam (not to be confused with the south outlet dam—Pawtuckaway Lake has outlets at both the north and south ends).

Camping at Pawtuckaway State Park is limited to the southern end of the lake, where there is a large campground and day-use area. To get there from the north, follow Deerfield Road back to Route 156. Drive south on Route 156 for 4.0 miles to Mountain Road. Turn right here, following signs to the park, which is approximately 2.0 miles up this road. If you're coming from the south, follow Route 156 approximately two miles north from Route 101, turn left on Mountain Road, and follow signs to the park.

There is a day-use fee for the park, which has a canoe launch area, public beach, picnic area, playground, and rest rooms. There are two camping areas: Horse Island, with eighty sites, many of which are on the water; and the mainland, with eighty-three sites, about a dozen of which are on the water. Other than campsites, this side of the lake is undeveloped all the way around to Neal's Cove, and there are some very pretty islands to explore in here. You will never feel very remote at the southern end of the lake, however, because of all the houses across the lake and the large number of motorboats in use during the summer months and on weekends. I much prefer the northern end of the lake for canoeing.

There are numerous hiking trails through Pawtuckaway State Park, including the Fundy Trail, which extends from the main park road near the picnic area up along Burnham's Marsh to the boat launch at the northern end of the lake. Farther west in the park, trails take you over several small mountain peaks, along a unique boulder field of glacial erratics, and into Round Pond. Pawtuckaway State Park is extremely popular during the summer months. In fact, there are often waiting lines to get into the park. If you can visit in September, though, this is a great spot. For information on camping and trails, contact the park (Pawtuckaway State Park, 128 Mountain Road, Raymond, NH 03077; 603-895-3031).

Great Bay
Durham, NH, and other towns

Great Bay is a large tidal estuary in southeastern New Hampshire near Portsmouth. Though located near heavily populated areas, most of the shoreline is undeveloped or only sparsely developed, and because of its shallowness and the variable water level, there are very few motorboats on it. Most of the bay is within the Great Bay National Estuarine Research Reserve, which includes more than four thousand acres of tidal waters and mud flats and some forty-eight miles of high-tide shoreline. The northeastern corner of the bay, on land occupied by Pease Air Force Base, is being turned into a National Wildlife Refuge—New Hampshire's first.

Because of tidal influences, Great Bay is quite unlike any other body of water covered in this book. It is a constantly changing place, with the shoreline migrating in and out twice daily with the changing tides. At high tide, Great Bay is more than twice as big as it is during low tide. While the constant change makes it a great place to explore—one where you could spend many days canoeing—some special precautions are in order. If you're not careful, you could easily get stranded on mud flats as the tide goes out. And if you don't plan your timing carefully, you may find yourself paddling against strong tidal currents.

With most lakes, and especially the larger ones, the paddler has to contend with winds coming up. At Great Bay, you have to plan around both wind and the tides. Paddling against the tidal current is like paddling upstream on a fairly swift river—believe me. Strong winds, which are common on the bay, can make paddling even more difficult. So in planning your visit to Great Bay, get hold of a tide chart, which will tell you when high and low tides will be.

Because Great Bay is so large, there are dozens of places to explore. Among the best are Adams Point (which provides the best access to the planned National Wildlife Refuge), and the Squamscott River inlet. To get into Great Bay from the boat launch on the northern side of Adams Point, you need to paddle around the point separating Great Bay from Little Bay. Because this channel is quite narrow, tidal currents can be very strong. If possible, plan a trip from the Adams Point launch into Great Bay as the tide is coming in, and your return as the tide is going out. This way you'll always have the current with you. If you do not know when high and low tides are, you can usually tell whether the tide is coming in or going out by looking at which way the

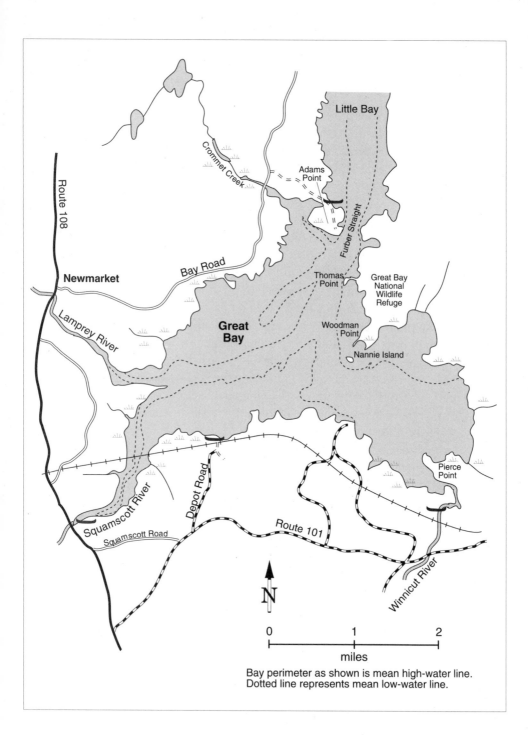

Bay perimeter as shown is mean high-water line.
Dotted line represents mean low-water line.

boats moored at Adams Point are facing. The boats face upstream, so if the tide is going out they will face south, and if the tide is coming in they will face north.

From Adams Point, you can paddle across the Furber Straight to the planned Great Bay National Wildlife Refuge. The eastern shore along here has picturesque bluffs overlooking the bay, with stands of large red pines above and rocky seaweed-covered coves below. Woodman Point at the southern tip of the Wildlife Refuge is spectacular. There's a trail leading out to the point, which overlooks Nannie's Island, where common terns (a state-listed endangered species) nested as recently as 1980. Be careful of poison ivy, which is particularly lush at Woodman Point and Thomas Point.

You can also paddle around Adams Point, and explore the western shoreline southwest toward Newmarket. At high tide you can paddle into Crommet Creek, but be aware that this area is exposed mud flat at low tide. During the winter months bald eagles roost along this shore and across at the Wildlife Refuge. The shoreline and shallows south of Adams Point have the most productive oyster beds in New Hampshire, and this is often one of the only areas in the state not closed to oystering because of pollution. If you put in at Adams Point and get caught fighting the tidal current getting back to your car, keep close to shore, where the current will be a lot weaker.

Another interesting area to explore is along the Squamscott River inlet into the bay. Except for the Squamscott River channel, though, this entire south side of the bay is exposed mud flat during low tide. Again, time your trip carefully.

At Great Bay and the surrounding salt marsh areas, you can expect to see a wide range of shorebirds (lesser yellowlegs, glossy ibis, snowy egret, American bittern, and green heron, to mention just a few), numerous species of ducks, cormorants, gulls, geese, and others. In the water, you're likely to see horseshoe crabs, hermit crabs, oysters, and ribbed mussels. Depending on wind and how clear the water is, you can paddle over the shallows and watch for marine life hiding among the prolific eelgrass. For those interested in fishing, three different species of sea-run salmon are caught here: Atlantic, coho, and Chinook (consult the book *New Hampshire Fishing Maps,* DeLorme Mapping Co., for choice fishing locations) along with various saltwater fish.

GETTING THERE: To reach the Adams Point boat access, drive north on Route 108 to Newmarket. Just after crossing the Lamprey River, turn right and drive 3.9 miles on Bay Road to the entrance to Adams Point and Jackson Lab (the gate here is nearly always open, I

Changing tides on Great Bay offer unique challenges for the quiet water paddler. Here is the shoreline across from Adams Point at low tide on an unusually still morning.

am told). The boat launch is 0.8 mile in on the left. There is parking for five or six cars at the launch, and room for a few more in a parking area just before the access. (For birders, there is an excellent spot for wading birds just on the other side of the road from this boat launch.)

The boat launch into the Squamscott River is off Route 108 just south of the bridge. Be careful turning off here, as the access road is in poor shape. You can also launch your canoe into this area by driving to the end of Depot Road. From the intersection of Routes 101 and 108 North, drive 1.7 miles east on Route 101 and turn left onto Depot Road. Drive in about a mile, turn left at the T, and park across the tracks. Parking is extremely limited here, but the state is planning to greatly expand the public access facilities with a larger parking area, trails, and an estuarian interpretive center.

If you're thinking of visiting Great Bay in the fall, note that the area is heavily used for waterfowl hunting. Check the dates of the hunting season before planning your trip and, if possible, avoid dates when hunters will be present. To find out the dates of hunting seasons in New Hampshire, contact the New Hampshire Fish and Game Department, 2 Hazen Drive, Concord, NH 03301; 603-271-3212.

Central
New Hampshire

Grafton Pond
Grafton, NH

Grafton Pond is one of those relatively unknown gems that you'll want to come back to again and again. Though small (235 acres), the lake seems much larger, owing to the many rocky islands, deep inlets, and hidden marshy areas near most of the inlets. One could spend several days exploring all the nooks and crannies of this lake and hiking some of the old logging roads around it. A large portion of the surrounding land is owned by the Society for the Protection of New Hampshire Forests, which is one of New Hampshire's most effective organizations involved in land preservation. There are a few houses on the western tip, near the dam, but these don't distract too much from the remoteness of the lake—probably because it's so easy to get out of view of them.

Grafton Pond is a natural lake that has been enlarged and deepened with a dam. The maximum depth is sixty-six feet and the water is quite clear. The shoreline is generally rocky and heavily wooded with mixed hardwood and conifers. Close to the water the conifers seem prevalent (balsam fir, red spruce, white pine, and hemlock), while farther in from shore red maple, white birch, and other hardwoods dominate. Geologists will enjoy the granite outcroppings found throughout most of the lake, some of which have sizable mica crystals, while birdwatchers may want to stay closer to the shallow-water marshy areas. There are wonderful grassy picnic sites on the islands and peninsulas jutting out into the lake. You will find some old camping sites, though camping is no longer permitted on the islands or around the lake perimeter.

Grafton Pond is a tremendous spot for wildlife. There were at least two pairs of loons on the lake in 1991. With the relatively safe islands

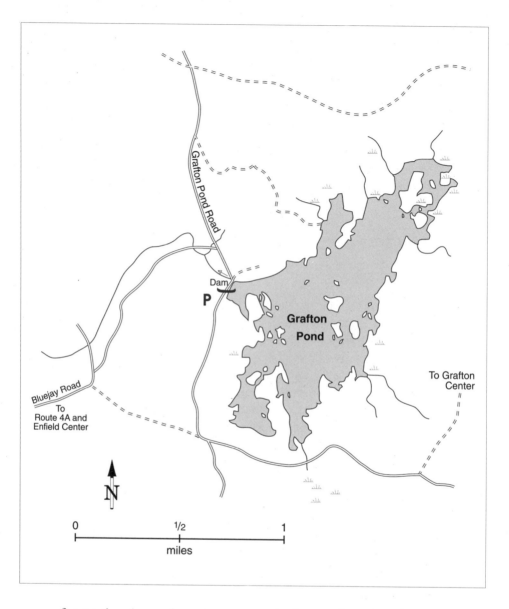

for nesting (away from raccoons and other predators) and a plentiful food supply, this has always been a great spot for them. During a late-April visit, I also saw quite a few wood ducks, an osprey (probably migrating through), and an assortment of more common lake and pond birds of the region: black ducks, mallards, great blue herons, kingfishers, and others. There are a number of active beaver lodges, especially along the northern shore, and I'm sure otter and mink also make this their home.

Grafton Pond has a good reputation for smallmouth bass. Pickerel, yellow perch, and horned pout are also caught here. A prohibition of motors larger than six horsepower keeps the pond relatively quiet, and more enjoyable for the dedicated angler or paddler.

GETTING THERE: The lake is accessible from Grafton Pond Road, which can be reached from Bluejay Road off Route 4A, approximately 2.2 miles south of Enfield Center. Drive approximately 0.8 mile on Bluejay Road and bear right at the fork onto Grafton Pond Road. Drive another 0.8 mile and turn right; you will reach the dam in about 0.2 mile. At the dam there is a small boat ramp and parking space for two cars on the lake side of the road and another eight or ten across the road.

For more information on Grafton Pond, contact the Society for Protection of New Hampshire Forests, 54 Portsmouth St., Concord, NH 03301; 603-224-9945.

Grafton Pond's deep coves and numerous islands offer plenty of opportunity for exploring and bird watching.

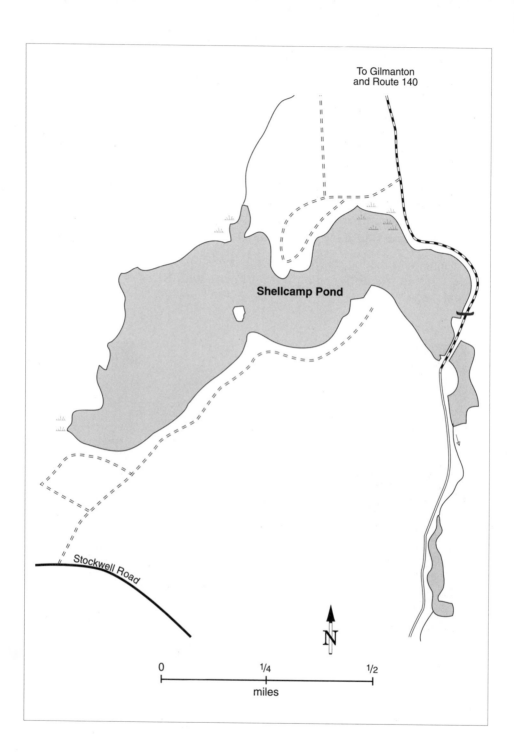

Shellcamp Pond
Gilmanton, NH

In the big-lake region of Winnipesaukee, with its big boats and big wakes, Shellcamp Pond is different. Though whitecaps were kicking up on Winnisquam and Winnipesaukee on the day we visited, Shellcamp was almost still. You might see a few motorboats on this small pond, and there are several dozen summer and year-round houses along the shore—especially along the southern edge—but for the most part this is a quiet, cozy, well-protected pond that a canoeist can enjoy for a pleasant afternoon of bass fishing or relaxed paddling. White pine is the dominant tree along the shore, with lots of red maple mixed in.

GETTING THERE: The best put-in point on Shellcamp is a small public boat ramp on an unmarked road leading south from Gilmanton. From the intersection with Route 107 in the center of Gilmanton, take Route 140 West for a couple of hundred yards, then turn left (south). You will reach the pond in 1.0 mile and see the boat access about 0.2 mile farther along the edge of the pond. The boat ramp is on the right side of the road beneath a beautiful stand of white pine trees, just before the creek passes under the road in a series of culverts. Parking is limited. If there isn't room for your car, you can drive a little farther down the road across the outlet and park by a large expanse of exposed granite.

The most remote part of the pond is to the north of the launch site. There is a fairly deep inlet that is quite marshy and full of birds. Even at the end of May, there was a veritable symphony of bird songs as we paddled along the northern shore. In the marshy areas, you're likely also to hear a chorus of frogs. The pond vegetation can get pretty thick, though, which restricts paddling by midsummer. To find out about the dates of duck-hunting season, contact the New Hampshire Fish and Game Department, 2 Hazen Drive, Concord, NH 03301; 603-271-3212. There are also some duck-hunting blinds in this part of the pond, so you would do well to keep away during duck-hunting season. There is a nice island on the pond that is thick with high-bush blueberries. Though I haven't been here in the late summer, I suspect that one could develop quite a belly-ache after an hour or two on the island!

All in all, this is a pleasant alternative to some of the larger, more popular lakes in this part of New Hampshire, especially on a windy day.

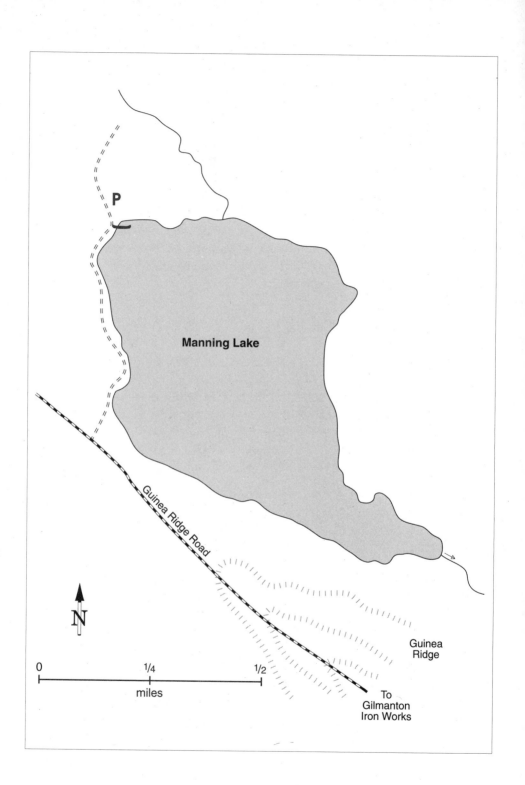

Manning Lake

P

Guinea Ridge Road

Guinea Ridge

To Gilmanton Iron Works

N

0   1/4   1/2
miles

Manning Lake (Guinea Pond)
Gilmanton, NH

Manning Lake, a few miles south of Lake Winnipesaukee in central New Hampshire, stands out for its crystal-clear water and sandy bottom along much of the shoreline. It is one of the cleanest-looking lakes I've visited in the two states. Freshwater mussels are numerous in the sand, evidence that the water really is quite pure. There are only about a dozen houses along the lake, and there were no other boats when I visited on an otherwise busy Memorial Day weekend. You will find a well maintained public boat launch, with plenty of room for parking, on the northwestern tip of the lake, near the end of a dirt road leading from Guinea Ridge Road.

Manning Lake, also known as Guinea Pond, is small (just over two hundred acres), and you can paddle leisurely around the perimeter in a couple of hours. Of course, you should plan for a lot more time if you want to try a little bass fishing or enjoy some swimming. In the early morning or late evening, you're likely to see a beaver or two, and perhaps an otter. Unfortunately, there is no camping on the lake.

Manning Lake's setting is simply gorgeous: it's nestled between Guinea Ridge on the south and the much taller Belknap Mountains on the north. Though located just a few miles as the crow flies from Lake Winnipesaukee, Manning Lake drains to the south instead of into the big lake. Unlike the vast majority of lakes in Vermont and New Hampshire, Manning is totally natural. The shoreline is heavily wooded with white pine, hemlock, red oak, basswood, and red maple. Right on the shore, you'll find some witch hazel, a fascinating low-growing tree that blooms in the late fall, and high-bush blueberry. Some stretches of shoreline are dotted with large granite boulders, though vegetation comes right down to water's edge around most of the shore. The sandy bottom drops off quite rapidly in some areas, reaching a maximum depth of fifty-six feet. Fish species caught here include smallmouth and largemouth bass, pickerel, yellow perch, and horned pout.

GETTING THERE: To get to Manning Lake, take Route 140 West from Alton. In the town of Gilmanton Iron Works, turn right onto Mountain Road (approximately 5.4 miles from Route 11), then take a fairly immediate left fork. Drive about three miles on this road, passing along with heavily built-up western shore of Crystal Lake, then take the left fork onto Guinea Ridge Road. Continue along Guinea Ridge Road for about 1.8 miles, and turn right onto an unmaintained road; you will reach the boat access in less than 0.5 mile.

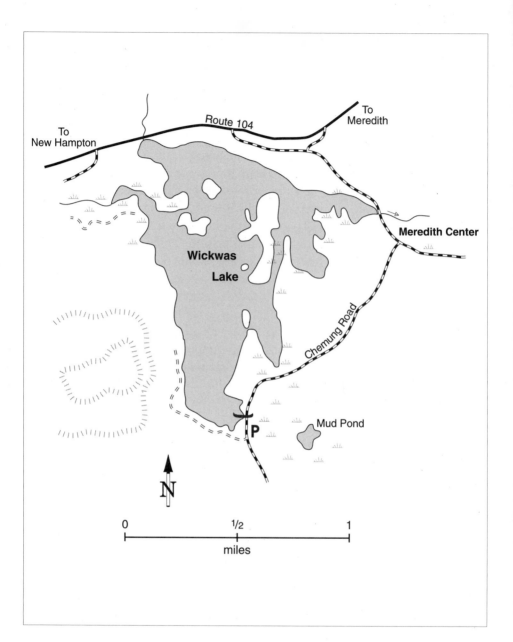

Wickwas Lake
Meredith, NH

If it weren't for the considerable development around parts of the shoreline and the motorboat traffic, Wickwas Lake would be one of the best canoeing lakes in New Hampshire. It's still pretty nice, especially once you get over the realization that there are no longer any truly pristine bodies of water in the New Hampshire Lakes Region. Wickwas offers lots of shoreline variation, a number of beautiful islands, several marshy inlets to explore, and a reputation for excellent bass fishing. The shores are heavily wooded with white pine, hemlock, and various hardwood species.

GETTING THERE: Wickwas Lake is just south of Route 104, between New Hampton and Meredith. To reach the best launching point, take Chemung Road southwest out of Meredith Center for a little over a mile to a sandy landing with plenty of space for parking on both sides of the little-travelled road. If you're coming from the west on Route 104, turn off toward Meredith Center (you can see the lake from the road) and take the first paved road to the right, Chemung Road.

Most of the development is along the southern arm of the lake near the public landing, though the northern shore of the lake along Route 104 also has a few dozen houses on it. The most remote part of the lake is the eastern section, especially in the deep inlet behind the large island. We were just barely able to paddle around the marshy eastern side of the island in late May; with a lot more pond vegetation or a slightly lower water level, that channel would not be navigable. On the other side of the island, there is a pleasant picnic spot in a stand of tall red pines on a point of land extending into the lake.

Wickwas Lake is large enough (328 acres) for a full day of relaxed exploring. There is no camping on Wickwas, but Pemigewasset Lake is just a few miles farther west on Route 104 and has a large private campground, Clearwater Campground, next to the lake (campsites are not actually on the lake, but you can store a canoe at no charge next to the boat dock). There is currently no public boat access to Pemigewasset Lake, so you have to be a registered camper to get onto the lake. For information, contact Clearwater Campground at RFD 1, Box 123, New Hampton, NH 03256; 603-279-7761.

White Oak Pond

Holderness, NH

Of the small Lakes Region ponds, White Oak is my favorite. For starters, outboard motors larger than 7$1/2$ horsepower are prohibited. As a result, the lake seems much less oriented toward motorboats. The few houses along the shore have small docks with canoes on racks, instead of huge docks jutting out into the lake with behemoth powerboats tied up waiting to be released. The 291-acre lake seems tranquil and relaxed. I saw only one other boat on the pond when I visited on Memorial Day weekend, and that was a solo canoe.

GETTING THERE: To reach White Oak Pond, drive west on Route 25 and 3 from the bridge in Holderness for 1.8 miles. If you are coming from the east or southeast on Route 25 and 3, the pond is approximately 6 miles from Meredith, where Routes 25 and 3 come together. The public boat launch is just off the main road (on the south side of the road), where College Road splits off. The boat ramp is small and sandy, just right for putting in a canoe. Parking is limited, with room for only six to eight cars.

About a dozen houses dot the shoreline, primarily along the northeastern shore and the western end. Most of these are quite unobtrusive and have obviously been there for a long time. There are several islands, including one that is quite large. Like the surrounding land, these islands are privately owned.

The eastern end of the pond is very marshy. At least in the late spring, it is possible to paddle quite far up the inlet creek, winding through the cattails, old beaver lodges, mossy hummocks, and thick marsh habitat—ideal for all sorts of birds. I paddled a quarter- to a half-mile up this inlet and was struck by its peacefulness. There are no houses in sight, and the only sound is the singing of warblers, marsh wrens, and red-wing blackbirds.

Out on the main lake we watched a pair of loons—from a fair distance, of course, so as not to disturb them. The shoreline is heavily wooded with white pine, red oak, red maple, and a few stands of hemlock. (Only after quite a bit of looking did I actually find a white oak, and that was a rather sickly specimen; this is pretty far north for white oaks). I was also struck by the variety of ferns around the lake: huge stands of royal and cinnamon along the shore, and dense carpets of various wood ferns farther up on the banks.

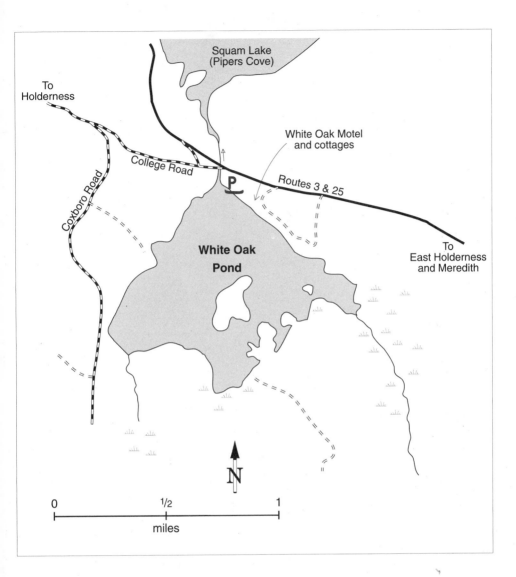

There is no camping on White Oak Pond, but there is a motel with lake-front cottages for the paddler who wants (and can afford) the comfort. The White Oak Motel is fairly expensive during the peak summer months, and the lake-front cottages tend to be full, but off-season the rates drop considerably and lake-front cottages are more likely to be available. For information, contact the White Oak Motel, RFD 1, Ashland, NH 03217; 603-968-3673.

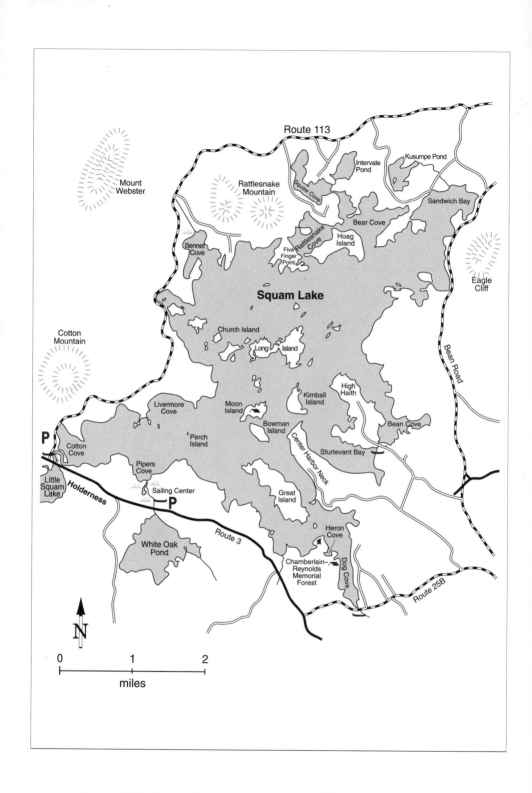

Squam Lake

Holderness, NH

Squam Lake is one of New Hampshire's real treasures, and it's one of my favorite lakes for an extended visit. Though very large (6,765 acres), the lake is highly varied, with dozens of islands, deep coves, and marshy inlets to explore. One could easily paddle every day for a week and still not explore its entire sixty-one-mile shoreline and islands. The water is clean and crystal clear with sandy white beaches, ideal for swimming. Squam Lake, the setting for *On Golden Pond,* is not without its drawbacks, however. There is a fair amount of development around the shoreline and on many islands, and motorboat traffic can be heavy during the summer months. Weekend boat traffic can be particularly heavy and last well into the evening. (Be very careful and carry a bright flashlight to flash at oncoming motorboats, if you're thinking of a moonlight paddle.)

You should also be aware that Squam Lake is large enough to be quite dangerous to the inexperienced canoeist. Strong winds can come up quickly and generate waves large enough to swamp a canoe. The wake from a big motorboat can amplify the wind-formed waves, compounding the problem. To reach some of the islands, including Moon Island, where camping is available, you may have to cross a mile or more of open water. Use great caution on Squam, and be ready to alter your plans if weather conditions are adverse.

The shoreline and islands of Squam are heavily wooded with mixed hardwood, white pine, red pine, and hemlock. You will see a few unusual species, such as sour gum, whose leaves turn a brilliant crimson early in the fall, and some huge, ancient specimens of the more common trees. In the marshy coves you'll find buttonbush, with its unusual round white flowers, and there are beautiful stands of mountain laurel on some islands and peninsulas.

Because most of the islands and surrounding land are privately owned (though the water itself is public), you may want to concentrate your exploring in three primary areas where there are natural areas open to the public: Five Fingers Point, Chamberlain-Reynolds Memorial Forest, and Moon Island.

Five Fingers Point, on the northern shore of the lake, is owned by the University of New Hampshire and offers deep coves with sandy beaches, marshy inlets, and forest trails to explore. From here you can hike up to the two steep knolls known as the Rattlesnakes that overlook the lake. West Rattlesnake has an exposed rock outcropping, visible from most of Squam, that offers a superb view of the lake. (If you don't want to hike all the way up from Five Fingers Point, you can drive to a trail head on Route 113. From the intersection with Route 3, drive 5.5 miles north on Route 113 and leave your car in a parking area on the left [west] side of the road. Cross the road and walk 100 feet or so back toward Holderness to find the trail head. From here it's about a mile up to West Rattlesnake lookout, about a half-hour hike.)

Rattlesnake Cove and Squaw Cove, to the east and north of Five Fingers Point, are fairly well protected from wind and the only parts of Squam Lake that are off-limits to water-skiing. Portions of Hoag Island, in this part of the lake, are open to picnicking, though overnight camping and fires are prohibited.

The Chamberlain-Reynolds Memorial Forest, adjacent to Dog Cove at the southern part of the island, is owned by the New England Forestry Foundation. Two camping areas in the forest are managed by the Squam Lake Association. There is a great network of trails in this area, including a raised boardwalk trail through the swamp. The area is alive with birds, and some of the hemlock and pine trees in the forest are over two feet in diameter and more than three hundred years old. There are two docks here, one on each side of Heron Cove, and a very nice, though heavily used, beach around the peninsula from Heron Cove.

Heron Cove, like a number of other small, shallow coves around Squam Lake, may be off-limits to boaters during May through July to protect nesting loons. Nesting loons can easily be disturbed by people, whether on foot or in a boat (see page 51). Please respect the "Loon Nesting Sanctuary" floating signs that you will see at this time of year.

Moon Island, near the center of the lake, is a great spot for day use and overnight camping (see page 47). There are several trails on the island, including an interpretive wetlands-ecology trail at the northeastern end.

Many other islands and shoreline areas are just as beautiful as these public-use areas and—remarkably—most are not posted with no-trespassing signs. Nonetheless, I recommend you stick to the more-public areas described above. Few property owners have marred the shoreline with private-property signs. As long as we are careful not to abuse or deface the private land, perhaps those shoreline trees can remain free of signs. Of course, this is not to say that we can abuse the public access areas. The Squam Lake Association, the New England Forestry Foundation, and the University of New Hampshire could easily restrict the use of their properties if littering, damage to vegetation, or violation of established rules became a problem.

The author and family, fully loaded and on their way out to Moon Island on Squam Lake.

Camping on Squam Lake

The Squam Lake Association maintains several camping sites on the lake: two near the southernmost tip of the lake in the Chamberlain-Reynolds Memorial Forest, and two on Moon Island near the center of the lake. There is a small fee for camping ($2 per person per night in 1991), and reservations must be made in advance with the Squam Lake Association (P.O. Box 204, Holderness, NH 03245; 603-968-7336). If you plan on doing much canoeing here, it would be a good idea to buy a copy of the *Squam Lake Chart*, published by the Association. It is printed on waterproof material and is available at a number of area stores, as well as through the Squam Lake Association. The lake is just too large to present an accurate picture of it in a one-page map.

The Heron Cove site is the most isolated of the camping sites. It is on a point of land above the small cove, nestled beneath tall hemlocks and white pines, carpeted with soft pine needles, and ringed with mountain laurel and blueberry bushes. There is a composting toilet at the site, a fire ring, a small dock, and room for several tents (total capacity fifteen people). Because of the surrounding marshy area, you can reach the campsite only by boat.

Flipping bannock for breakfast while camping at Moon Island on Squam Lake.

Across Heron Cove and around a peninsula is the large Deerwood Shelter, with a capacity of fifteen and room for additional tents nearby. You can hike or boat into Deerwood Shelter. Less than fifty yards from the shelter is a sizable beach that is heavily used during the summer months—most people get there by motorboat. Both the Heron Cove and Deerwood Shelter camping areas are within the Chamberlain-Reynolds Memorial Forest, owned by the New England Forestry Foundation, but the campsites are managed by the Squam Lake Association.

The most exciting camping spot for the serious paddler, though, is Moon Island. The island was purchased by the Squam Lake Association in 1986 and is open for public use. There are two tent sites, both on the western end of the island. The first is larger and more open (and nearer to the outhouse), with room for five or six tents. The second has room for only two or three tents, but it is closer to the dock and the water and tends to be breezier and less buggy. Both sites are within an easy walk to several of the beautiful beaches. In addition to these two campsites, there is also a day-use fireplace site on Moon Island—on the western end of the island, roughly between the two campsites. Though you must be careful paddling to this island, it's a great place for kids—our two- and five-year-old daughters had a fantastic time during a four-day stay.

GETTING THERE: Access to Squam Lake is relatively limited, which is one reason the lake is so attractive. In Holderness, the free public access point is a boat ramp on the Squam River along Route 113, very close to the intersection with Route 3, opposite the entrance to the Science Center of New Hampshire. (The Science Center is a great place to visit, especially with children. For information write the Science Center of New Hampshire, Route 113, Holderness, NH 03245, or call 603-968-7194.) There is a public parking area right across the road from the boat ramp. Overnight parking is not permitted, but campers staying at one of the Squam Lake Association campsites can park behind the Curry Place in Holderness.

In Center Harbor you can park on Route 25B near the tip of Dog Cove and carry your boat down to the water. While the carry is short (about 50 feet), the trail is steep, there are no facilities of any kind, and parking is limited along the road. Some people also launch canoes at the Center Harbor Town Beach in Sturtevant Bay, parking on the south-

You can view most of Squam Lake from West Rattlesnake Mountain. The trail starts from Five Fingers Point near the northern end of the lake.

western side of the road on the mainland side of the small bridge. Swimming here is limited to Center Harbor residents.

Another parking possibility, though you have to pay for it, is the Sailing Center at the Olde Colonial Eagle Motel along Route 3, about two miles east of Holderness. In 1991 the fee for parking here and launching a boat was $10. This motel is on the inlet into Pipers Cove and is the closest access point to Moon Island—about two miles across open water. The Sailing Center also offers canoe rentals. For information write The Sailing Center on Squam Lake, U.S. Route 3, Holderness, NH 03245, or call 603-968-3233.

The Loon
Voice of the Northern Wilderness

No animal better symbolizes wilderness than the loon, whose haunting cry resonates through the night air on our more remote northern lakes. The bird seems almost mystical, with its distinctive black-and-white plumage, daggerlike bill, and piercing red eyes. But like our remaining wilderness, the loon is threatened. As recreational pressures on our lakes and ponds have increased, the loon has been pushed farther away. Protecting this bird is a responsibility that all of us who share its waters must take on.

Along with being a symbol of northern wilderness, the common loon, *Gavia immer,* is one of the most unusual birds you will ever encounter. It is a large diving bird that lives almost its entire life in the water, visiting land only to mate and lay eggs. Loons have a very difficult time on land because their legs are positioned quite far back on their bodies, behind the center of gravity, preventing them from walking—a fact that plays heavily in its threatened status.

Loons are remarkably well adapted to water. Unlike most birds which have hollow bones, the loon's bones are solid, enabling them to dive to great depths. They also have internal air sacs, which they can compress or expand to control how high they float in the water. By compressing these sacks, a loon can submerge gradually (like a submarine) with barely a ripple, or swim along with just its head above water.

Their heavy bodies make takeoff from the water difficult. A loon may require a quarter-mile of open water to build up enough speed to lift off, and it may have to circle a small lake several times to build enough altitude to clear nearby hills or mountains. On occasion a migrating loon will mistake a highway for a body of water and crash-land, injuring its feet. The loon will be unable to take off again unless it is brought to a large-enough body of water. When migrating, a loon flies rapidly—up to ninety miles per hour—but cannot soar.

Loons generally mate for life and can live for twenty to thirty years. The female lays two eggs in early May and both male and female, which are indistinguishable, take turns incubating the oblong, mossy-green eggs. If the eggs are left unattended, the embryos can die in just half an hour. Because loons cannot walk on land, the nests are always very close to shore—where a passing motorboat or canoe can scare the birds away. Loons often nest on islands, where raccoons and skunks are less likely to find and devour the eggs. On some lakes and ponds you will see floating nesting platforms built by concerned individuals or organizations to improve the

chances of nesting success. On reservoirs with varying water levels, these platforms are especially important, because they rise and fall with the water level, preventing the nests from being flooded or stranded.

Loon chicks are fully covered with black down, and they usually enter the water a day after hatching. Young chicks may be seen riding on a parent's back, but they grow quickly on a diet of small fish and crustaceans. By two weeks of age, they are already half the size of the adult and can dive to relatively deep lake bottoms and cover more than thirty yards under water. Loon chicks remain totally dependent on their parents, however, for about eight weeks, and they do not fly until ten to twelve weeks of age. After a chick leaves the nest, it will not return to land for three or four years, when it reaches breeding age and returns from the sea—where loons winter and where young loons mature.

Loon nesting in New Hampshire and Vermont has been only moderately successful in recent years. According to surveys conducted in 1991, there were 102 nesting pairs in New Hampshire, producing 85 surviving chicks. In Vermont, where the loon is listed as endangered by the state, there were only 15 nesting pairs and 14 surviving young. As development encroaches on our lakes and as recreational use increases, loons are increasingly at risk.

Because loons can easily be disturbed when nesting, it is extremely

Watch for signs indicating loon nesting habitat, and keep away from these areas from May through July. This area on Little Averill Pond has been protected by the Vermont Nature Conservancy.

important for paddlers to keep their distance and be aware of warning displays during the nesting season of early May through mid-July. (If a nest fails, the loons may try up to two more times. The later the chicks hatch, however, the lower their chance of survival.) If you see a loon flapping its wings and making a racket during the nesting season, it probably has a nest or young chicks nearby. Paddle away from shore. Canoers can be a serious threat to nesting loons, because both loons and paddlers prefer the shallower protected coves and inlets. If a nesting site is marked with buoys or warning signs, as is done on many lakes and ponds, always respect those signs and keep your distance.

Loons have lived in this area longer than any other bird—an estimated sixty million years. Let's make sure this wonderful species is still around for our future generations to listen to on a still, moonlit night. For more information on loons, and to find out how you can help protect them, contact the Loon Preservation Committee in New Hampshire, (RR 4, Box 240 E, Meredith, NH 03253; 603-279-5000), or the Vermont Institute of Natural Science, P.O. Box 86, Woodstock, VT 05091; 802-457-2779. You might also want to find a copy of the excellent *The Loon: Voice of the Wilderness,* by Joan Dunning.

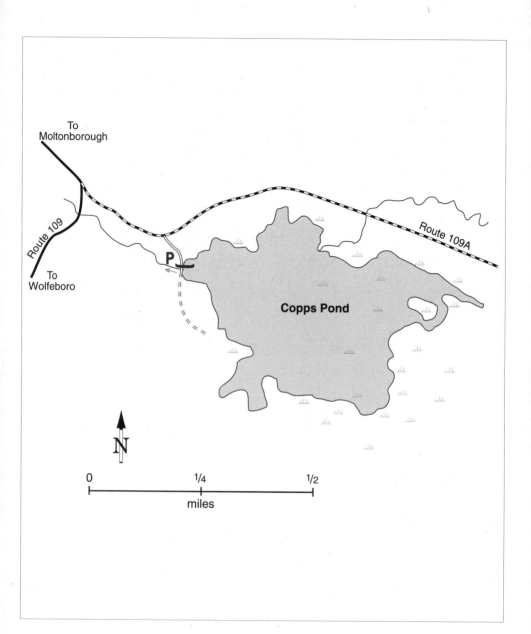

To
Moltonborough

Route 109

To
Wolfeboro

Route 109A

P

Copps Pond

N

0   1/4   1/2

miles

Copps Pond
Tuftonboro, NH

This is really more of a marsh than an open pond, but it's a great spot for birdwatching and plant identification. By mid-July about 80 percent of the surface of this small pond is covered with vegetation, including three different species of waterlilies (water shield, fragrant waterlily, and bullhead lily), pickerelweed, sedges, rushes, and cattails. We also saw beautiful (and relatively rare) rose pogonia orchids and sundew plants on floating sphagnum mats. There are a number of wood-duck nesting boxes around the pond, which is a superb habitat for numerous species of waterfowl.

GETTING THERE: Copps Pond is very close to Moultonborough Bay on Lake Winnipesaukee and accessible from Route 109A, about 0.2 mile from the turn off from Route 109. After turning east on 109A, look for a fairly quick right turn onto a dirt road. Follow this a short way to the small parking area for Copps Pond Marsh, maintained by the New Hampshire Fish and Game Department.

The 208-acre wildlife management area, including 168 acres in marsh and open water, is used for hunting during waterfowl season, so plan any canoe trip to avoid the hunting season. Fishing is said to be good, especially for horned pout and brook trout. For information on the waterfowl hunting seasons in New Hampshire, contact the New Hampshire Fish and Game Department, 2 Hazen Drive, Concord, NH 03301; 603-271-3212.

There is no boat ramp, so you should have no motorboats to contend with, and the only development on the pond is a New Hampshire Highway Department building and storage sheds on the northern side, along Route 109A. In this region of New Hampshire, with the many deep, clear lakes dotted with vacation homes, Copps Pond provides a pleasant alternative, especially on a windy day when you want a smaller, more protected spot.

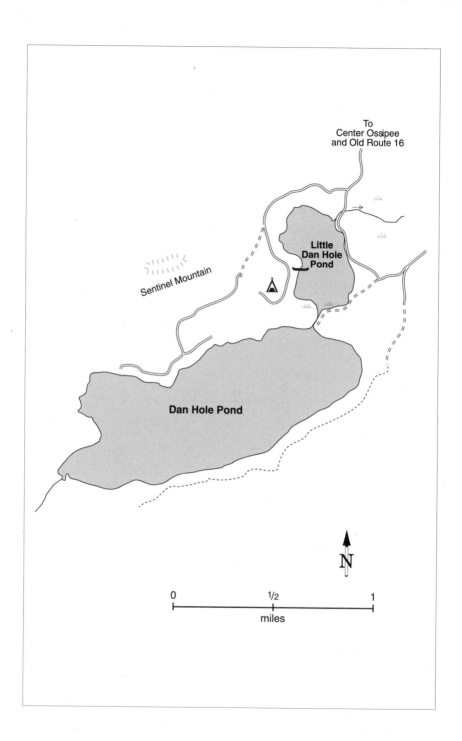

To
Center Ossipee
and Old Route 16

Little
Dan Hole
Pond

Sentinel Mountain

Dan Hole Pond

N

0   1/2   1

miles

Dan Hole Pond and Little Dan Hole Pond
Ossipee, NH

The family that wants to spend some quiet time away from the hustle and bustle of Winnipesaukee and Squam, the big lakes that dominate this part of New Hampshire, may enjoy Dan Hole Pond and Little Dan Hole Pond. The water is crystal clear, sandy beaches provide excellent swimming, and the heavily wooded shores are only lightly developed. Gasoline-powered motorboats are prohibited from Little Dan Hole Pond, and jet-skis are prohibited from both ponds. I saw one loon on Big Dan Hole Pond and suspect they nest here.

Access to both ponds is limited, however. The only public access I could find is through the Terrace Pines private campground, and that is limited to overnight campers ($20 per night for a family in 1991) and their guests (at an extra day-use charge). Terrace Pines has sites on both Big and Little Dan Hole Ponds, and the waterfront sites on Little Dan

Pickerelweed in the shallow water of Little Dan Hole Pond near the connecting brook to Big Dan Hole Pond.

Waterlilies and pickerelweed surround a half-submerged boulder on Little Dan Hole Pond.

Hole are especially pleasant. For details, contact Terrace Pines Campground, P.O. Box 98, Center Ossipee, NH 03814; 603-539-6210. The campground generally operates from mid-May through mid-October. Rental canoes are available.

Fishing at both ponds is good. Big Dan Hole Pond, which is very deep, is known for its salmon and lake trout, while the smaller pond, with horned pout and pickerel, is a great spot for the beginning angler. There is a dam between the two ponds, but the carry is very easy and just a few hundred feet. From Big Dan Hole Pond the portage path is obvious: carry down the dirt road from the dam to a path that leads down to the water in Little Dan Hole. If you're coming up from the smaller pond, the take-out spot is harder to find. Look for a path on the eastern side of the inlet in the marshy area. You may need to walk up to the dam and follow the path down to locate the take-out point, or you can just carry it up along the stream as we did. Be careful about strong winds on Big Dan Hole Pond—they can be dangerous.

GETTING THERE: To get to the Dan Hole Ponds, follow signs for Terrace Pines Campground from Old Route 16 in Center Ossipee.

White Lake

Tamworth, NH

This is a great choice for families looking for a pleasant camping spot where the kids can learn about canoeing on a quiet, relatively safe lake. White Lake is small (120 acres) and fairly round, with most of the shoreline visible from most locations, so it provides a good place for beginning paddlers to have a go of it without parents. The swimming beach is perhaps the best in the White Mountains, with clean white sand, a lifeguard on duty during heavy use times, and plenty of shallow water for young children. The six-horsepower restriction for motorboats helps keep noise down. The lake, beach area, and campground are all within White Lake State Park, and there is no other development on the lake. Most of the shoreline is heavily wooded but with relatively little undergrowth, enabling one to pull up for a picnic lunch very easily.

The lake itself is quite shallow. It was formed as the glaciers retreated during the last ice age. Geologists say that a large chunk of ice was left buried in the glacial till as the glacier receded, and as it melted it left a natural depression that filled to form the lake. An easy trail extends around the lake, offering plenty of views of the lake (the walk can be pretty slow going during blueberry season, though!). One of the

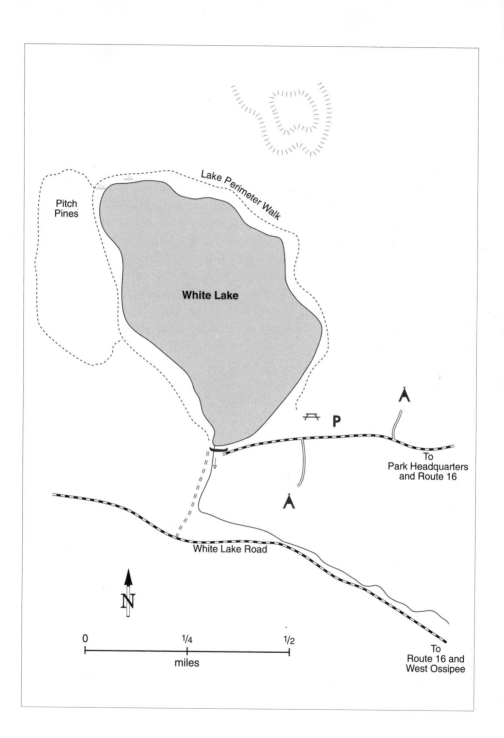

Pitch
Pines

Lake Perimeter Walk

White Lake

P

To
Park Headquarters
and Route 16

White Lake Road

N

To
Route 16 and
West Ossipee

0   1/4   1/2
miles

most interesting attractions is a stand of unusually large pitch pine (*Pinus rigida*). Some of these trees are more than two feet in diameter, and the area is recognized as a National Natural Landmark. Though commercial use of pitch pine is limited today, early settlers in the area probably used the durable, decay-resistant wood for fenceposts and mill wheels. Pitch pine rarely grows to the size of the trees seen here. The pitch pine are located throughout the park, but the greatest concentration is a 72-acre stand on the northwestern end of the lake that has a side trail passing through it. The Pitch Pine trail also passes by the small Black Spruce Ponds (not canoeable), which are classic bogs with such species as northern pitcher plant and sundew.

GETTING THERE: To get to White Lake, take Route 16 north from West Ossipee. White Lake Road, the road into the park, is about 1.5 miles from the intersection of Routes 16 and 25 West, and it is well-marked. There are fees for both day use and camping. Day use rates for 1991 were $2.50 per person, with children twelve and under free. Coupon books of day passes and season passes are also available. There are three camping locations in the park with over 180 sites, including a few right on the water. Nineteen ninety-one camping rates were $14 per site for a family and $7 per extra adult. Lake-front sites are more expensive. During off-season, the park is open for day use with no facilities. For information contact White Lake State Park, Box 273, West Ossipee, NH 03890, or call 603-323-7350.

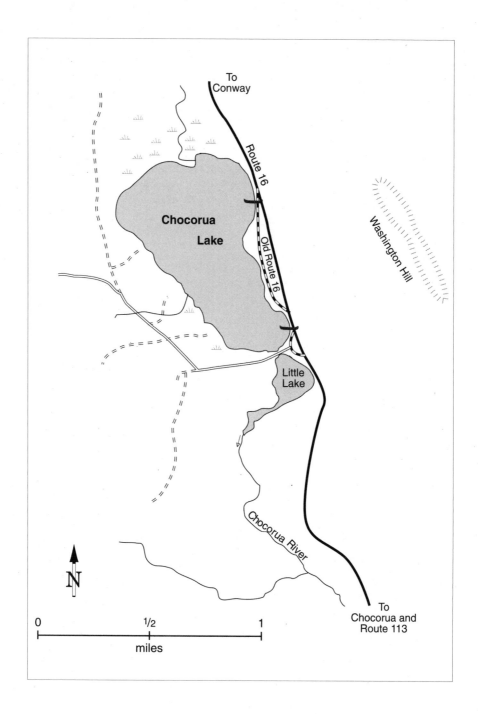

To
Conway

Route 16

Chocorua
Lake

Old Route 16

Washington Hill

Little
Lake

Chocorua River

N

To
Chocorua and
Route 113

0   1/2   1

miles

Chocorua Lake

Tamworth, NH

Chocorua Lake is a pleasant spot for a morning or afternoon of canoeing. Nestled beneath Chocorua Mountain, one of New England's most picturesque and most photographed mountains, the 222-acre lake is off-limits to outboard motors, so the only noise you'll have to deal with is from Route 16, which runs along the eastern side of the lake. At the southern end you can canoe under a little bridge to get into adjoining Little Lake, which is smaller and more protected but has a few more houses around it than the large lake.

For the birdwatcher, there are several nice marshy areas to explore on Chocorua Lake, and more extensive marshy areas and two beaver lodges on Little Lake. The entire eastern side of the lake is conservation land and open to the public. You can park and put in anywhere along old Route 16, which runs between new Route 16 and Chocorua Lake, and has plenty of room for picnicking. There are one or two outhouses on this conservation land, and a great picnic area with big granite slab tables and wooden benches built into the large pine trees near the passage between the two lakes. All along this edge of the lake are

A small bridge separates Little Lake from Chocorua Lake. Chocorua Mountain is visible from almost anywhere on the two lakes.

huge white pine, red pine and red oak trees. Brook trout fishing is supposed to be quite good at the lake inlet and outlet.

Beware of strong winds that can come out of the mountains from the northwest, creating hazardous conditions. Watch for clouds building near the craggy peak of Chocorua Mountain, which can be a sign of gale-strength winds to follow.

GETTING THERE: The lake is readily visible from Route 16 a little over a mile north of the town of Chocorua (where Routes 16 and 113 intersect). Driving north, take a sharp left-hand turn near the northern end of the lake to get on old Route 16, which is one-way south.

Conway Lake
Conway, NH

This large, 1,300-acre lake just south of the White Mountains offers some excellent canoeing with its varied and lightly developed shoreline, marshy coves, and islands. On a breezy day, one would do best to stick to the southern end, which forks into two long and relatively narrow fingers. There is no development on the smaller, southwestern finger, and just a half-dozen houses on the larger, more easterly inlet. Both provide marshy shelter for herons, various ducks, beaver, and other wildlife. I watched a deer drinking at the water's edge and startled a great horned owl early one August morning at the southwestern tip. In the wider inlet I was joined by a pair of loons and, judging from the fresh tracks I saw in the mud near the southern boat access, I just missed seeing a moose.

The western side of the lake most of the way up to the northern end has numerous deep marshy coves to explore and very little development, except around the one road near the southern fork and at the northern end. Be aware that the northern half of the lake is quite wide, and strong winds can come up quickly. While some of the coves are well protected, you can reach them only by canoeing out on the open lake.

GETTING THERE: There is a large public boat access at the lake outlet on the northern end. From Route 302, take Mill Street south and drive 0.8 mile. The put-in point is on the right, and parking is on the

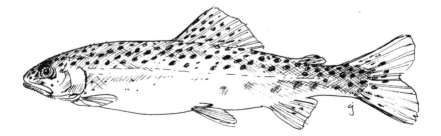

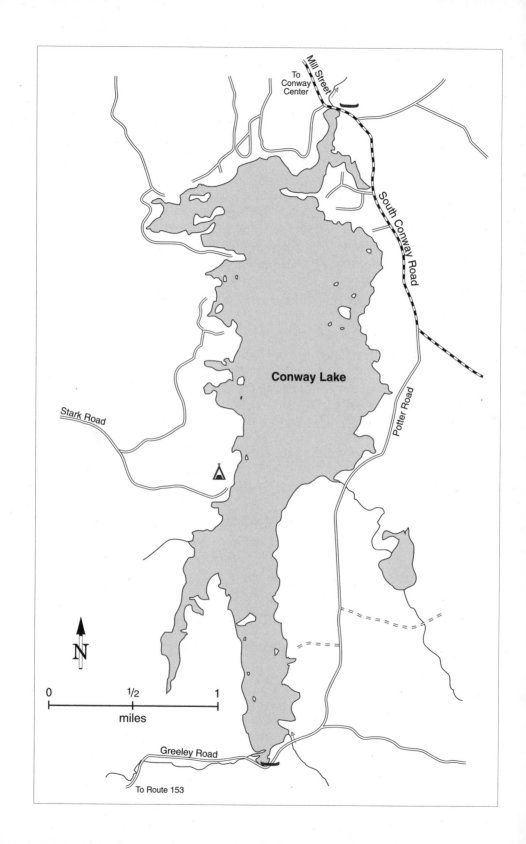

left. If you're interested in a pleasant walk, there's a trail from the parking area with interpretive signs describing the several generations of water-powered mills that existed here. Near the ruins of the most recent mill building, you can still see metal hoops from the old wooden sluice, or penstock, scattered in the creek. At the southern end of the lake, near the primary inlet, there is a hand-launch area along Greeley Road (unpaved) with parking for a half-dozen or so cars. Greeley Road can be reached via Route 153 about a mile north of Eaton Center.

Cove Camping Area, a private campground, is on the western side of the lake just above the fork near the southern end. While most campsites are not right on the lake, the campground provides easy access to Conway Lake and to other lakes in the area (see sections on Chocorua Lake and Upper Kimball Lake). Canoes can be rented from the campground office. For more information or to make reservations, contact Cove Camping, P.O. Box 778, Conway, NH 03818; 603-447-6734.

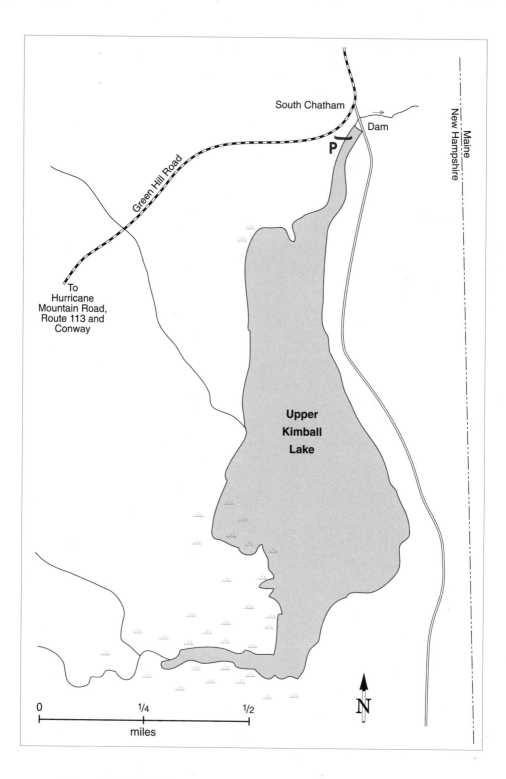

Upper Kimball Lake
Chatham, NH

Right next to the Maine border in the southeastern corner of New Hampshire's White Mountains lies Upper Kimball Lake. Upper Kimball is a small (about 150 acres) and narrow body of water with a carry-in boat access at the northern end next to the dam. The northern section has a number of houses on it, but most are set back somewhat from the water making them less noticeable. My favorite part of the lake is the southern end and inlet, which winds through a boggy marsh that is rich in birdlife and interesting flora.

One can paddle in at least a half-mile through thick stands of pickerelweed, several species of waterlily, sedges, reeds, cattails, and floating mats of sphagnum dotted with the unusual sundew plant. Cranberries, sweetgale, various heaths, alder, and buttonbush are established where they have been able to get a foothold in the gradually filling fen. On solid ground along the shoreline, the most common trees are red maple and white pine. Even in mid-August, the birds seemed to be everywhere: tree and barn swallows dancing over the water, redwing blackbirds and cedar waxwings flitting among the pickerelweed blooms, sparrows hopping around the old beaver lodges, and warblers dining on insects in the maple trees. Bring your binoculars and field guides for a great day of exploration!

GETTING THERE: To get to Upper Kimball Lake, you can take Hurricane Mountain Road east from Route 16 in North Conway. Hurricane Mountain Road initially follows the Conway-Bartlett town line, then the narrow winding road takes you up over Hurricane Mountain and down to Green Hill Road (6.1 miles). Turn left onto Green Hill Road at the T and go another 2.0 miles. You will see Upper Kimball Lake at a sharp left-hand turn at the bottom of a hill. There is parking at the put-in point for six or seven cars. Alternately, if you're coming from the south and want to avoid the horrendous factory outlet and mall traffic between Conway and North Conway, take Route 113 to East Conway, then turn left on Green Hill Road right next to the Maine border.

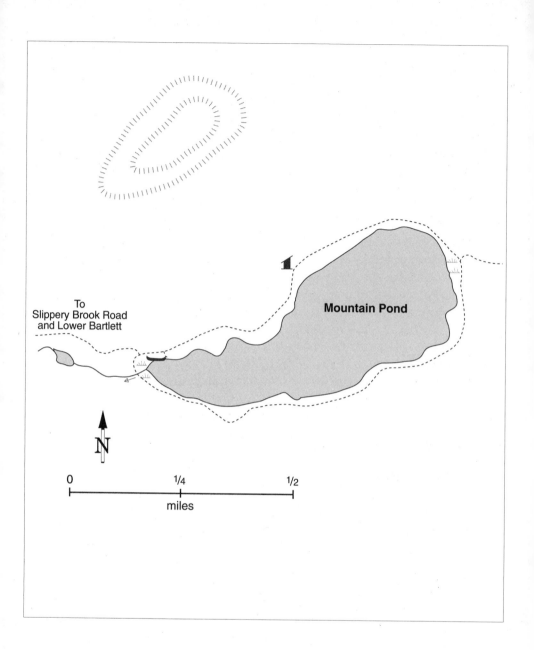

Mountain Pond

To
Slippery Brook Road
and Lower Bartlett

N

0   1/4   1/2
miles

Mountain Pond

Chatham, NH

Mountain Pond is the most remote of the canoeable ponds in White Mountain National Forest. Following a long drive up a winding, mostly unpaved road, you still have a carry of about one-third of a mile to the pond itself. But it's worth the effort if you appreciate out-of-the-way places, and it's beautiful even on a drizzly, foggy day. On the northern side of this totally natural pond, along the perimeter trail, there's an Adirondack shelter for those looking for secluded lakeside camping, especially before Memorial Day and after Labor Day, when visitation is low. You can also pitch a tent anywhere in this part of White Mountain National Forest.

For specific regulations on primitive camping in the National Forest, contact Forest Supervisor, White Mountain National Forest, P.O. Box 638, Laconia, NH 03247; 603-528-8755. Always use minimum-impact camping practices when away from organized campgrounds, as outlined in the White Mountain National Forest brochure on backcountry camping, or described in more detail in the book *Soft Paths* (Stackpole Books, 1988).

The vegetation around Mountain Pond is predominantly white pine, spruce, balsam fir, and white birch, with a dense undergrowth of blueberries and other shrubs. Because of the thick understory growth, there aren't many places where you can easily pull the canoe up and get out. Paddling around the 124-acre pond, you'll find a beaver lodge and a small marshy area at the outlet on the western end, where you might see a great blue heron or a few ducks. I saw two pairs of loons on the pond in 1991, but no young with either pair. Be careful not to disturb nesting loons.

GETTING THERE: To get into Mountain Pond, take Slippery Brook Road northeast from Lower Bartlett. If you're heading north on Route 16, turn right just after crossing the East Branch of the Saco River onto Town Hall Road, which turns into Slippery Brook Road. After 2.6 miles the steep, winding road turns to dirt, and you reach the parking area for Mountain Pond after a total of 6.7 miles. From the parking area, you need to carry in approximately 0.3 mile (ten to fifteen minutes) along a wide though potentially soggy trail. When you get to the loop trail (marked by a sign) turn left, and within 100 yards or so you'll see a trail to the right leading down to a nice put-in point. By continuing along the loop trail you'll reach the Adirondack shelter.

If you're an angler, try your luck for some brook trout, which inhabit these waters.

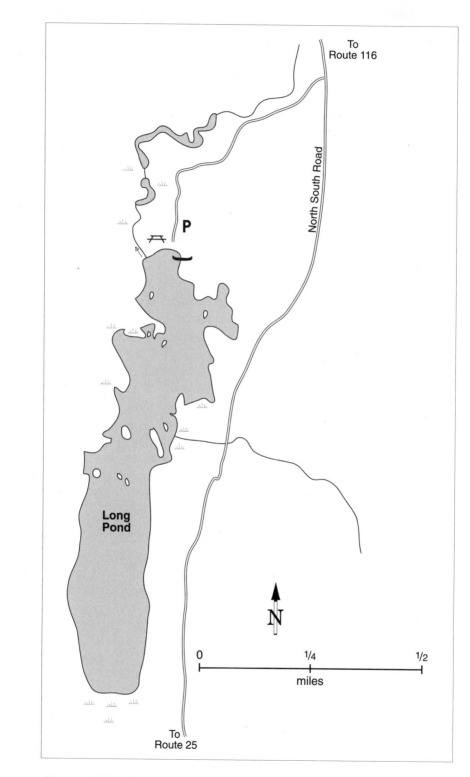

To
Route 116

North South Road

P

Long
Pond

N

0   1/4   1/2
miles

To
Route 25

Long Pond

Benton, NH

Accessible only by gravel road, surrounded by the White Mountains, and totally free from development, Long Pond is spectacular—it's one of my favorite bodies of water in the two-state region. Though relatively small (124 acres), the pond feels much larger, owing to its long profile, highly varied shoreline, and islands. The access is at the northern end, where there is also a small picnic area. While my five-year-old daughter and I were having breakfast there on a crisp September morning (after camping at Russell Pond, a half-hour away), we watched an otter playing fifty yards away. It's the kind of place where you could sit for hours just absorbing the peacefulness and beauty.

The northern half of the pond has a dozen or so islands to explore and marshy coves along the shoreline that provide rich wildlife habitat. While some of the shoreline is marshy—particularly at the southern end—most is wooded, with tall spires of fir and spruce mixed with deciduous trees such as red maple and yellow and white birch. A dense growth of viburnums, alders, and other shrubs makes shore access quite difficult along much of the wooded perimeter, but there are some rocky areas where you can disembark for a picnic lunch.

Paddling around the pond, you'll see a couple of beaver lodges. Try to get here early in the morning if you want to see beaver, otter, and mink. Though I did not see loons here, it seems like prime loon habitat. In the spring, be sure to avoid areas loons might use for nesting, and heed their warning calls (see page 51).

There is no camping on the islands in Long Pond, but primitive camping is permitted in the surrounding area. Family camping, replete with such luxuries as running water and showers, is available a few miles away at the Wildwood Campground on Route 112, or, if you prefer camping near water, at the Russell Pond Campground further east and south. For information on family campgrounds and regulations on primitive camping, contact White Mountain National Forest, P.O. Box 638, Laconia, NH 03247; 603-528-8755.

GETTING THERE: To reach Long Pond from the east or southeast, get off Interstate 93 at Exit 32 and drive west on Route 112. Approximately 11 miles from I-93, Route 116 joins Route 112 from the east. A mile farther, Route 116 South splits off to the left. Turn onto Route 116 South. After 1.6 miles turn left onto North South Road (unpaved) toward Long Pond (there is a sign for Long Pond). After 2.4 miles turn

Long Pond offers the finest canoeing in the White Mountains. Keep an eye out for otter, beaver, loons and other wildlife here.

right, again following the sign for Long Pond, and you will reach the picnic area in 0.6 mile.

If you are coming from the west or from I-91 (Exit 17), take Route 302 East through Woodsville, then turn onto Route 112 East. Follow Route 112 until you get to a sharp right turn onto Route 116 South, then follow directions as above.

Long Pond can also be reached off Route 25 from the south. Follow a paved road north from Glencliff, then turn left onto the unpaved North South Road 1.0 mile north of Route 25. Drive 4.1 miles on this road, then turn left onto the Long Pond access road.

Long Pond is the largest body of water that is a part of the White Mountain National Forest (though some larger lakes, with private cottages around them, are surrounded by National Forest land) and it is certainly one of the most beautiful. I consider it the best spot in the National Forest for canoeing. Information on trails in the area is available from the National Forest (address above).

Northern
New Hampshire

Umbagog Lake
Errol, NH

With bald eagles, ospreys, and peregrine falcons gracing the skies, loons filling the air with their haunting wail, and moose grazing on the thick shoreline vegetation, Lake Umbagog is the ultimate wilderness lake—in New Hampshire and Vermont, anyway. The 7,850-acre lake, with dozens of islands and more than forty miles of shoreline in both New Hampshire and Maine, is the most remote of the big lakes included in this guide. And unlike many of the better-known wilderness lakes in Maine and the Adirondacks of New York, Lake Umbagog (pronounced *umBAgog*) is readily accessible to the backcountry canoe-camper, with thirty wilderness sites around the lake managed by Umbagog Lake Campground. There are a few private cottages and camps on parts of the lake and some motorboat traffic, but for the most part the lake is very remote.

GETTING THERE: There are several ways to get onto the lake with your canoe. The only public boat launch area on the lake itself is at the southern end, off Route 26. Backcountry campers can also park and put in at the Umbagog Lake Campground, just east of the public boat launch. Closer to the northern end, canoers can put in on the Androscoggin or Magalloway River. For those planning to leave their cars, the Androscoggin access is a better choice. From Errol, head south on Route 26 and turn left onto a dirt road just 100 yards or so after crossing the bridge over the river. If you look carefully, you'll see a sign "Access to Public Water," at the turnoff. Follow the road about a mile and park at the end. From here, the main lake is about three miles up the Androscoggin. Although you'll be paddling against the current, it's an easy paddle along the slow-flowing, meandering river. Paddling toward

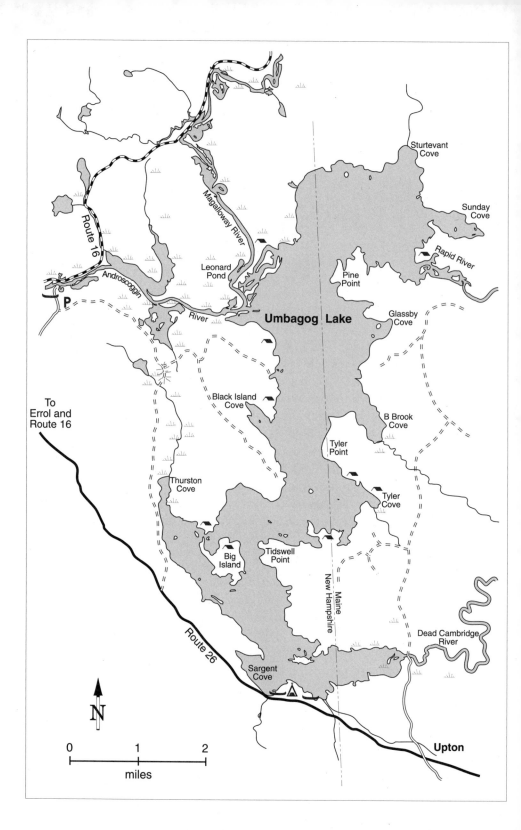

Sturtevant Cove

Sunday Cove

Rapid River

Route 16

Magalloway River

Leonard Pond

Pine Point

Umbagog Lake

Glassby Cove

Androscoggin

River

P

Black Island Cove

B Brook Cove

To Errol and Route 16

Tyler Point

Thurston Cove

Tyler Cove

Big Island

Tidswell Point

Sargent Cove

New Hampshire

Maine

Dead Cambridge River

Route 26

N

Upton

0   1   2

miles

Umbagog, there are a number of marshy ponds both to the right and left that you can explore if you wish. Keep an eye out for otter here.

You can also put in on the Magalloway River north on Route 16 from Errol. There are a number of pull-over places where a canoe can be launched along Route 16 (you'll find one 4.7 miles north of the Routes 16 and 26 intersection in Errol). The Magalloway provides a great starting point for paddlers who are being dropped off, but I did not find good places to park a car overnight along Route 16. The Magalloway is even more serpentine in its path than the Androscoggin, with numerous oxbow ponds and marshes where the wide loops of river eventually got cut off by short-cut channels. You are quite likely to see moose along here.

The lake itself is so large and so varied in its shoreline, I hardly know where to begin describing it. Umbagog is very shallow—its name means shallow water—with an average depth of only fifteen feet. There are many marshy areas that provide ideal nesting habitats for such duck species as hooded mergansers, common mergansers, black ducks, and wood ducks. You will see lots of nesting boxes that are used by both wood ducks and hooded mergansers (see page 17 for information on wood ducks). The largest marshy area—called Leonard Pond—near the northwestern corner of the lake is an extensive thick, grassy marsh, which counts as its residents New Hampshire's only nesting bald eagles (in a large pine tree on an island where the Magalloway flows into Umbagog), and lots of nesting ospreys. (On all of Umbagog there are more than 20 nesting pairs of osprey!)

Everywhere on the lake you will see loons, and you will hear their call on most spring and summer evenings. In 1991 there were fifteen nesting pairs of loons on the lake, which raised thirteen chicks (a relatively low success rate), and there are said to be as many as fifty to sixty loons total. During May, June, and July be particularly careful not to disturb nesting loons. Even a quiet paddler inadvertently getting too close to a nest can result in the adults abandoning it, and loons always nest very close to the water (see page 51).

My favorite places on the lake include Leonard Pond, the coves along the inlet of the Rapid River on the northeastern end of the lake, and some of the small coves and islands along the shoreline east of Tidswell Point to the south. In the early morning light, in a cove just east of Tidswell Point, we watched three moose grazing by the water's edge, and each little cove along here seemed to have its own family of wood ducks, mergansers, or black ducks. Big Island, which was purchased by the Society for the Protection of New Hampshire Forests in

Umbagog Lake is beautiful on a quiet morning, but be aware that strong winds can come up quickly.

the 1980s, is an open woods of spruce and fir with so many years of accumulated needles that the ground seems to bounce as you walk. The island includes six campsites. The sites on the north shore of Tyler Cove (#21, #22, and #23) are particularly good for children because there is a protected sandy swimming beach at the end of the cove. Even the most developed part of the lake, the inlet of the Dead Cambridge River at the far southeastern end, is worth exploring. In fact, we got our closest look at a moose not 200 yards from a cottage near the mouth of the river (which is rocky and not canoeable, at least in the summer). Except for the far northern shore of the lake, most of the houses and camps are in the southern section, below and to the east of Big Island.

The vegetation around Umbagog Lake is quite varied. In some areas conifers—balsam fir, spruce, northern white cedar, hemlock, and white pine—predominate. Others have more deciduous trees, including yellow and white birch, red maple, and an occasional red oak. We saw a few relatively rare jack pines on the lake. I was surprised to see so few blueberry bushes here and absolutely no evidence of beavers anywhere on the lake.

In planning a trip to Lake Umbagog, be aware that it is a very large lake. Potentially dangerous winds and waves can come up very quickly, making open-boat paddling hazardous. Be ready to change your plans or— horrors—get ferried out to your campsite by the campground owners (for a fee). Paddling around the lake for two days in August, we got into heavy winds both afternoons, even though the water had been smooth as glass on both of those mornings. Wind blowing from the north across several miles of water can build up sizable waves.

There are lots of fish in Umbagog Lake, as evidenced by the large osprey population, but relatively few prime sports fish. My paddling partner during a mid-August trip pulled out yellow perch, smallmouth bass, and lots of fall fish (a large scaly species of minnow with a deeply forked tail), one of which weighed several pounds. In the deeper holes near the northern end you may hook a salmon, brook trout, or brown trout. Near the inlet of the Rapid River are the lake's deepest holes, a few of which are over fifty feet. This is where you might hook a salmon or trout. With the right bait, lures, or flies, you shouldn't have too much trouble pulling a few meals out of the lake.

In the northeastern section of the lake, you might also want to spend some time in Sunday Cove. There are some beautiful campsites here, including #14, located on an island.

For information on camping at Umbagog Lake or to make reservations, contact the Umbagog Lake Campground, P.O. Box 181, Errol, NH 03579; 603-482-7795. Their backcountry sites are not cheap ($16 per night for a family in 1991), but they're about the best thing going in

Early morning fishing on Big Island, near the southern end of Umbagog Lake.

New Hampshire and Vermont when it comes to remote lake camping (see also the section on Green River Reservoir in northern Vermont). When you contact the campground, ask for a map of the campsite locations. If you'll be paddling to the site with young children, be sure to note the scale of miles when you select a site. Even the closest sites are about two miles from put-in locations, and access from the southern end requires paddling across a sizable stretch of open water (on the north end, you can reserve a site near the mouth of the Androscoggin or Magalloway River to minimize paddling over open water).

Finally, you should know that efforts are afoot to protect the scenic beauty and unique environment of Umbagog Lake. The Society for the Protection of New Hampshire Forests has purchased Big Island, and much of the lake may soon be purchased by the federal government to become a National Wildlife Refuge. In October of 1991 Congress tentatively authorized $5 million for protection of the lake. Currently almost all the land around Umbagog Lake is owned by paper companies.

You are very likely to see moose on the shores of Umbagog Lake. This bull moose heads toward shore in a cove east of Tidswell Point.

First Connecticut Lake
Pittsburg, NH

First Connecticut Lake, like the other Connecticut Lakes (see sections on Second and Third Lake), is one of the jewels of northern New Hampshire. Though development has encroached around the shores of this lake more than Second or Third Lake, it still offers some superb wilderness paddling. In the more remote inlets at the northeastern tip and southern end in all but the busiest seasons, you're just as likely to see moose as people. For the angler, First Connecticut Lake is also considered one of the finest lake trout and salmon waters in New Hampshire.

Be forewarned, though, that First Connecticut is a very big lake (2,807 acres). The center of the lake is several miles across, and even a fairly gentle wind can generate some sizable waves across that distance. Some even argue that the lake is not appropriate for open-boat canoeing. I make it a rule to stick close to shore, always wear my life vest, and keep my plans flexible. If you've traveled a long way to canoe one of the big lakes in northern New Hampshire and it's just too windy, visit one of the smaller ponds instead (see sections on East Inlet, Scott Bog, and Third Connecticut Lake). Don't risk putting a canoe on First or Second Connecticut Lake if there's much more than a gentle breeze. Unexpected winds coming out of the southeast were so strong once as I paddled down the northern shore that I actually found myself surfing on the two-foot waves in my small solo canoe. The front third of the boat rose right out of the water as the large waves passed under me. Exciting perhaps, but potentially quite dangerous. Be careful!

GETTING THERE: A good access point to the lake is at the northeastern tip, where the Connecticut River flows in. If you've been camping at Deer Mountain Campground and are driving south on Route 3, continue 2.3 miles past the Second Connecticut Lake dam and turn left (southeast) onto a dirt road that is marked with a sign for the Magalloway Mountain lookout. (From the south, this turnoff is roughly 4.7 miles from the dam at First Lake.) Take this dirt road 1.1 mile to the timber bridge, which is your put-in point. There are some light rapids for the first couple of hundred feet downstream from this bridge (you can carry along shore if you wish), then the river opens up into a gradually widening arm of First Lake. This section of First Connecticut Lake—down to Greens Point—is open only to fly fishing.

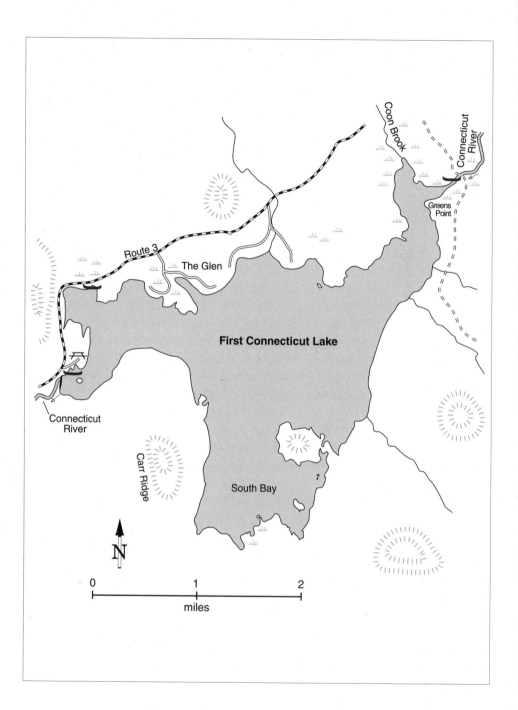

Coon Brook

Connecticut River

Greens Point

Route 3

The Glen

First Connecticut Lake

Connecticut River

Carr Ridge

South Bay

N

0   1   2

miles

If the weather looks promising and you're up for a lengthy paddle, you can travel down along the southeastern shore of the lake and explore the more remote sections of the lake. If the weather is uncertain or your time is limited, I'd suggest sticking to the northern shore, where you are more accessible to Route 3 and civilization.

The northern tip of the lake, including the Connecticut River and Coon Brook inlets, is quite marshy—good habitat for moose, beaver, deer and otter. You can paddle up Coon Brook a little way through the marsh and alder thickets until your progress is blocked by rocks. You can really feel the remoteness on this part of the lake, surrounded by thickly wooded spruce-fir forests and hearing the eerie cry of the loon. On an early morning with mist rising from the lake, moose browsing on pond weeds and birds singing from the wooded shore, you feel like you're in a different world.

The western arm of the lake, though not feeling quite as remote, is also very beautiful. You could spend a half-day just paddling around this end from the put-in near the dam, never even venturing onto the largest section of the lake. There is a small island near the dam, but during the loon nesting season from June through July, I'd suggest avoiding the temptation to visit this and other small islands lest you interrupt the loon's nesting (see page 51 for more on loons). There are a few other places where you can launch a boat along the more developed northern shore of the lake, on an access road off Route 3, but the western tip near the dam is the nicest, with picnic tables and outhouses maintained by New England Power Company, grassy fields, and a sandy beach area.

There are numerous logging roads to explore on foot or mountain bike in this area, though camping is not permitted without permission from the paper companies, which own most of the land in Coos County.

Average ice-out for First Connecticut Lake is early May.

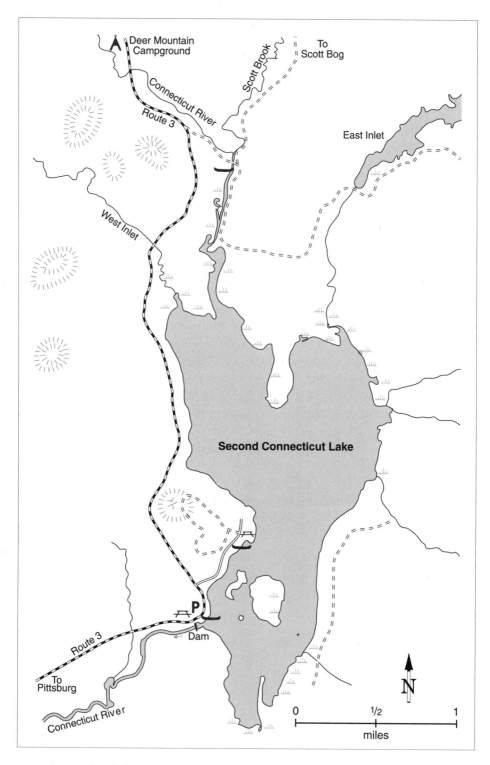

Second Connecticut Lake

Pitttsburg, NH

Second Connecticut Lake is one of my favorite big lakes in Vermont and New Hampshire. At 1,286 acres, it is less than half as large as First Connecticut Lake, and more manageable for the open-boat paddler—and there is much less development. Like First Lake, it offers almost endless exploring opportunities. The eleven miles of shoreline are highly varied, with lots of marshy inlets, especially at the northern and southern ends, and deep spruce-fir forests around most of the rest of the shoreline. At dawn and dusk you're likely to see moose grazing on pond vegetation in the various inlets, along with otter, mink, great blue heron, and various ducks. And you're almost certain to see loons, several pairs of which make Second Lake their home. Lake trout and salmon fishing are excellent in the lake.

GETTING THERE: A great place to put in for a day of paddling on Second Lake is at the northern tip where the Connecticut River (still more of a creek here) passes beneath a timber bridge on a dirt road, 1.0 mile from Deer Mountain Campground. To reach this access point, drive south on Route 3 approximately 0.6 mile from Deer Mountain Campground. Turn left onto an unmarked gravel road and drive 0.4 mile to a timber bridge—this is your put-in point.

The main boat launch for the lake, managed by the New England Power Company, is on the west shore just north of the islands, reachable from a well-marked access road off Route 3. You can also launch a canoe from a picnic area at the dam farther south, although this access requires a somewhat longer carry.

The Connecticut River joins Scott Creek just above the bridge. Paddle south on the gently flowing and gradually widening channel for about a mile until it opens into the main lake.

This entire northern end of the lake, including the main inlet and West Inlet, is fantastic for a paddler: thick, grassy marshes full of inlets to explore and dark green spruce and fir trees rising in sharp spires behind them. The water is clean, though slightly reddish brown from natural tannins. If you paddle around to the eastern, undeveloped side of the lake, you will pass a number of other similar inlets, each with its own secrets to reveal to the curious. Some sections of shoreline are gravelly or rocky, and you'll find a few sandy beaches, though much of the shore is quite marshy.

Near the southern end of the lake are two fairly large islands and one small one. As with all islands on remote lakes, be careful not to disturb nesting loons (see page 51).

Remember, Second Connecticut is a big lake. Be aware that winds can come up quickly and generate sizable waves. If you're planning a trip to this area, keep your plans flexible. If the winds are too strong, choose one of the smaller bodies of water instead of Second or First Lake (see sections on East Inlet, Scott Bog, and Third Connecticut Lake). And, as always on large lakes, wear your personal floatation device.

Camping on Second Lake is not permitted, but you can camp at state-operated Deer Mountain Campground, just north of the lake on Route 3. This is also known as Moose Falls Campground—I am told the name was changed to "Deer Mountain" when it was discovered that there are no falls anywhere in the area. Deer Mountain Campground has about twenty campsites, excellent spring water and outhouses, but there are no showers or other conveniences. There are also rental cabins and housekeeping cottages farther south on Route 3. For information on these, contact the North Country Chamber of Commerce: P.O. Box 1, Colebrook, NH 03576; 603-237-8939.

East Inlet
Pittsburg, NH

A moose was grazing belly-deep in water on the far shore of East Inlet when we drove in. Tree swallows skimmed the water surface, and a few families of black duck scurried for protective camouflage among the reeds at water's edge. Paddling next to the shore I could study the remarkable pitcher plants in full bloom, their odd reddish flowers on straight stems bowing over as if looking at the sphagnum moss beneath.

East Inlet, located in the northern tip of New Hampshire near the better-known Connecticut Lakes, has to be one of the most beautiful bodies of water I've ever set paddle to. It is small—just a few hundred acres in a long, sinewy channel—but truly wild and pristine. The shores are mostly marshy, with ancient, rotting stumps peering out from the brackish water and huge fields of reeds and sedge swaying in the breeze. Farther in from the water on solid ground are the deep green spires of spruce and fir that make up the northern boreal forest.

Paddling northeast from the dam, the wide channel continues for a mile or so. Then the lake turns to marsh and the inlet stream winds a serpentine pathway through the grassy marsh and thick alder swamp. Tamaracks join the spruce and fir trees along the shores at this end. Paddling through this marshy section, called Moose Pasture, it's hard to know which is the real channel and which is an isolated oxbow. As you paddle farther in, though, the deep channel becomes better and better defined. I must have paddled at least a mile up this creek with my solo canoe, which seemed barely short enough to make the tight turns in some places.

Canoeing here has an air of excitement to it, since you never know what might be around the next bend: beaver, a family of ducks, a lone moose. The farther up this inlet you canoe, the smaller the channel becomes, with the ever-present alders reaching out into the creek from both sides. Eventually, the alders totally block your passage and you have to find a place wide enough to turn around.

GETTING THERE: To reach East Inlet, drive south on Route 3 from Deer Mountain Campground approximately 0.6 mile and turn left (east) onto an unmarked dirt road. Cross a timber bridge after less than 0.5 mile and then take the right fork, which goes south for a little way along the northern tip of Second Connecticut Lake before veering away from the lake. (See also the map of Second Connecticut Lake on page 84). Follow this road approximately 1.6 miles to the dam at East Inlet, where you can launch your canoe. On a windy day, when rough water

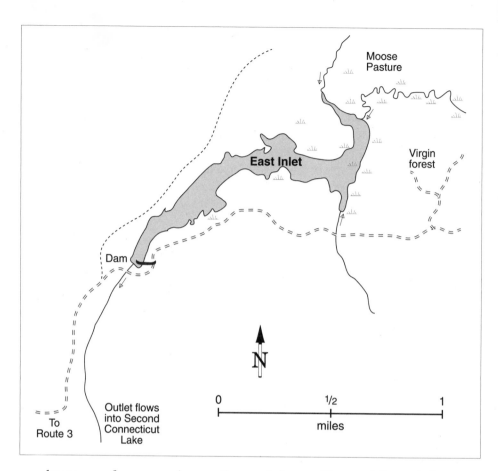

keeps you from canoeing on the much larger First and Second Connecticut Lakes, East Inlet is an ideal alternative—but it's nice anytime.

East Inlet is within the Norton Pool and Moose Pasture Natural Area, owned by the New Hampshire Nature Conservancy. Gasoline-powered motorboats are prohibited from this body of water. At the far end of the open water and across the alder swamp, there is a section of virgin spruce-fir forest, one of the only remaining stands of such forest in New England. You can apparently reach it by canoe and foot, but you'll get your feet plenty wet. There's a better access to the stand of virgin forest: continue driving past the East Inlet Dam for about 2.5 miles, then take the left fork. From there it's a rather difficult hike past the ruins of an old bridge. The old-growth forest will be on your left (to the west).

For more information on East Inlet, contact the New Hampshire Nature Conservancy, 2½ Beacon St., Suite 6, Concord, NH 03301; 603-224-5853. For information on camping and other area lodging options, see the section on Second Connecticut Lake.

Snapping Turtle
Hidden Pond Dweller

Snapping turtles are the most common species of turtle in our area, even more common than the painted turtle. In fact, they inhabit almost every beaver pond, millpond, lake, and marsh in New England. Some bodies of water are home to hundreds of snapping turtles, but you wouldn't know it.

Even if you spend quite a bit of time paddling around our ponds and lakes, you will only rarely see this largest of our turtles. Unlike the sun-loving painted turtles, snappers prefer the depths of the pond bottom and rarely bask in the sun.

The snapping turtle, *Chelydra serpentina*, is easy to recognize if you come across one, especially if it is out of water. They have long tails with spiny ridges and very large heads relative to the size of their bodies. The young have distinct ridges on the top shell, or carapace, though this is often worn smooth on larger adults. On the underside of the turtle, the bottom shell, or plastron, is very small and shaped like a cross. If you pick up a snapping turtle, be very careful. The safest way to pick it up is by the tail, holding the turtle well away from your body. I wouldn't mess with any large snappers.

Mature snapping turtles are large animals—though usually not as big as the wide-eyed estimates of enthusiastic observers. The carapace can reach a length of twenty inches (which means an overall length, nose to tail, of over three feet). A large turtle can weigh more than sixty pounds. This is by far the largest turtle species found in our area.

I occasionally see snappers underwater from my canoe, if the water is relatively clear and not too deep. On a few occasions I've seen them on the bank above a pond or slow-moving river—probably enroute to or from a nearby body of water, or perhaps about to lay a clutch of eggs. My usual glimpse of snappers, though, is just the triangular nose sticking out of the water ahead of me as I paddle along. At first I think it's just a waterlily leaf flipped over, but my binoculars tell me otherwise—if I have time to look before the nose submerges.

Many people are afraid of snapping turtles—and I'll admit I had a bit of concern when I watched two large snappers chasing one another just inches beneath my canoe on a shallow lake-edge in central New Hampshire—but they are really quite harmless, as long as they are in the water. Even if a snapper bites a swimmer's toe underwater, it quickly lets go, realizing that the quarry is more than it can handle. In the water, snappers are very shy and will avoid any human contact. The time to watch out for snappers is when they are on land. They will lash out with lightning speed if they feel threatened. A large snapper, with its massive jaw muscles and razor-sharp beak, exerts more than four hundred pounds per square inch of force with its bite—easily enough to sever a finger.

If you can look beyond their grotesque appearance and sometimes nasty disposition, snapping turtles are fascinating animals. They have been around for at least eighty million years and are believed to be the oldest reptiles in North America. Like all turtles, their rib cage and vertebrae have evolved into the bony carapace and plastron. While this shell offers armored protection for most turtles, the snapper's small plastron offers almost no protection to its underside. So for defense out of water, the snapper does just that: it snaps.

Most turtles hibernate for long periods during winter, but the snapping turtle is relatively resistant to cold. They can sometimes be seen swimming beneath the ice in the middle of winter, though in our climate they will typically hibernate in the bottom mud for awhile during the heart of winter. When idle underwater, a snapper does not need to surface for air. Special surfaces in its rear cloacal cavity can extract oxygen from the water, much as gills do. When active, though, the turtle needs more oxygen and must surface for air, and this is when the quiet paddler is most likely to catch a glimpse of one.

A snapping turtle's diet is composed of a wide range of animal and plant material, including fish, frogs, salamanders, occasional ducklings, dead animals, and aquatic plants. A snapper can kill anything its size or smaller, but it seems to prefer the easy meal. They have a superb sense of smell, which helps them scavenge for dead animals. Interestingly, this trait has on occasion been used to find human drowning victims. There is a story of an American Indian who found and retrieved drowning victims using a snapping turtle on a long leash. When released into the water, the turtle would unerringly head right for the decomposing corpse and latch onto it with its strong jaws, and its handler would reel it in—corpse and all.

A mature female leaves the water in late spring or summer to lay her eggs. She digs a hole and typically deposits from twenty to thirty (rarely, up to eighty) eggs the size and shape of ping pong balls, then covers the hole. In addition to this hole, she may dig several false holes to mislead predators, which take a heavy toll on snapping-turtle clutches. The eggs usually hatch in the fall, some seventy to 100 days after laying (depending on temperature), and the inch-long hatchlings make a beeline for the water— often to be gobbled up by raccoons, birds, and other predators.

Snapper populations are quite secure in New England, unlike those of most other turtles. They seem to tolerate current levels of environmental pollution and live in highly polluted marshy areas in our cities. Snapper meat is highly regarded, and in some areas snapping turtles are trapped heavily. Roads take less of a toll with snappers than with more terrestrial turtles.

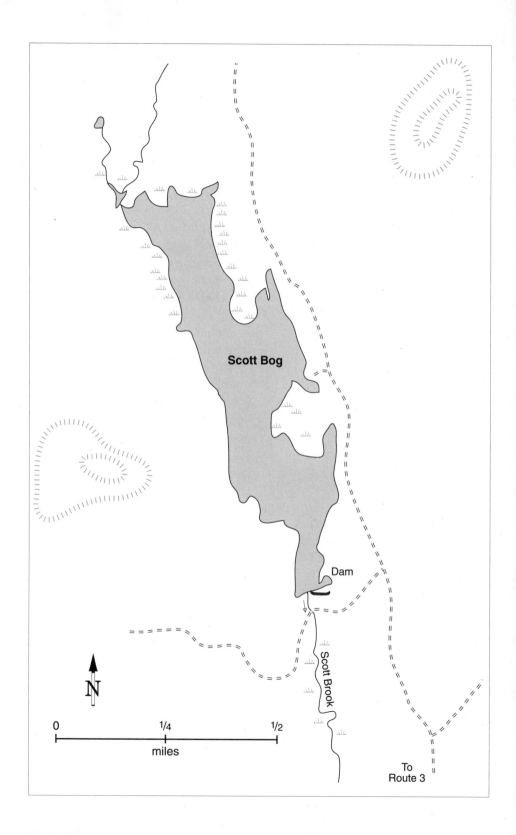

Scott Bog

Dam

Scott Brook

N

0   1/4   1/2
miles

To
Route 3

Scott Bog

Pittsburg, NH

Way in the northern tip of New Hampshire, along with the well-known Connecticut Lakes, are a few out-of-the-way bodies of water worth exploring. One of these is Scott Bog, located between Second and Third Connecticut Lakes. Scott Bog isn't easy to get to, but you aren't likely to see many other visitors. There is one cabin on the east side of the lake, leased from Champion Paper, which owns most of the surrounding land. (I don't know how often or how heavily this cabin is used.)

Scott Bog is a beautiful northern fen, with floating sphagnum mats, pitcher plants, alders, tamarack, and the surrounding spruce fir forests. The lake is shallow with a murky bottom. At the northern end is a beaver dam and many sun-whitened snags of old trees, left over from the dam construction. The marshy shores are full of wildlife and are ideal habitat for moose.

If high winds keep you off the larger Connecticut Lakes, Scott Bog is a good alternative. It is just a short drive from Deer Mountain Campground on Route 3, which has about twenty sites with spring water and pit toilets (see section on Second Connecticut Lake).

In the early morning hours you're very likely to see moose in Scott Bog and along the roads leading into it. Fishing at Scott Bog is restricted to fly and bait fishing (lures are prohibited).

GETTING THERE: To get to Scott Bog, drive south on Route 3 for 0.6 mile from Deer Mountain Campground (also called Moose Falls Campground). Turn left (east) onto an unmarked dirt road. You will cross a timber bridge after roughly 0.4 mile, then bear left at the fork and continue for another 2.5 miles, at which point you will come to a road going to the left. You should see a sign on a tree at this turnoff pointing to the dam. (See also the map of Second Connecticut Lake on page 84). Either park off the road near the turnoff or if the road is passable and you have the right vehicle, drive down it. The road to the Scott Bog dam was in very poor condition when I visited, and I didn't want to risk it, even with our relatively low-clearance four-wheel-drive car. Carry your canoe down this road a third of a mile or so, ford Scott Brook, and you will get to the dam and put-in point just ahead.

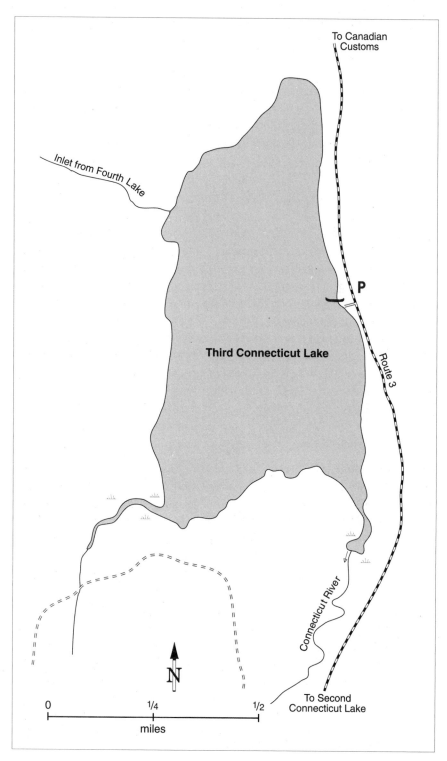

To Canadian
Customs

Inlet from Fourth Lake

P

Route 3

Third Connecticut Lake

Connecticut River

N

0   1/4   1/2

miles

To Second
Connecticut Lake

Third Connecticut Lake

Pittsburg, NH

Less than a mile from the Canadian border, in the northern tip of New Hampshire, lies Third Connecticut Lake. While not quite the headwaters of the Connecticut River (tiny Fourth Connecticut Lake, accessible only by foot from the Customs office at the border, is considered the headwaters), Third Lake might as well be. It is a small natural lake of 278 acres, beautifully nestled into the deep boreal forest of Coos County. The shoreline is entirely undeveloped, though you can find ruins of two structures just to the north of the boat launch area. The lake is very deep (maximum depth one hundred feet), which provides good lake trout fishing. Rainbow and brook trout are also found here.

Unlike the larger and better-known Second and First Connecticut Lakes, Third Lake has very little variety to the shoreline. There are few inlets to explore, and most of the shoreline is gravel. From the parking area and unimproved boat launch on Route 3, nearly the entire lake perimeter is visible, so if others are out on the lake in motorboats, it's hard to feel very remote in your canoe. Nonetheless, Third Lake is worth a visit, if for no other reason than to get out on the northwestern shore and step across the Connecticut "River"—just a couple feet wide—where it trickles into the lake. At the northern tip, there's also a nice sandy swimming beach.

If you want a real surprise, drive north on Route 3 from Third Connecticut Lake into Canada (Customs is only a mile away). As you cross the border, there is a sudden and dramatic change in the countryside. You leave the deep boreal wilderness forest of spruce and fir and enter into open farmland. The change is uncanny—you have to experience it to believe it.

At the U.S. Customs office, you might also want to pick up a little hiking map they provide and walk into the so-called Fourth Connecticut Lake. The walk takes you along the U.S.–Canada border, then down to the little pond—where the mighty Connecticut River (New England's longest and most important river) begins its 410-mile journey to Long Island Sound and the Atlantic Ocean.

GETTING THERE: Getting to Third Connecticut Lake is easy. Just drive north on Route 3, 4.2 miles past the Deer Mountain Campground. The lake and boat access will be on the left—you can't miss them. (If you're driving in a dense fog and get to the Canadian Customs office, turn around and drive about a mile south.) Driving along Route 3, watch out for moose—and for cars stopped in the middle of the road as the occupants watch moose!

The lake adjoins Connecticut Lakes State Forest, which runs along the Route 3 corridor. Camping is available about five miles south at the state-operated Deer Mountain Campground (also called Moose Falls Campground), which has about twenty fairly close-together sites, good spring water, and outhouses—see section on Second Connecticut Lake for more information on camping and other lodging opportunities in the area.

Southern Vermont

Sadawga Pond
Whitingham, VT

Sadawga Pond, located just above the Massachusetts border in Whitingham, Vermont, is one of the most unusual bodies of water you're likely to paddle on. The 194-acre pond has a floating island on it. The sizable island—about 25 acres—is covered primarily with sphagnum moss and other fen vegetation, although there are also some tamaracks as tall as twenty feet growing on it. According to a 1952 article in *Vermont Life*, this is the only honest-to-goodness floating island in the Western Hemisphere and one of only two in the world (the other is in Switzerland).

Although the island—really several connected islands—floats, it is not free to sail around the lake like a raft. Roots tether it to the ground beneath the pond. Someone who lives near the pond told me that in shifting winds the island pivots a little, but that is usually the extent of its movement. The floating island was apparently formed in the early 1800s, when dams were constructed on the two outlets of the existing small pond. The original pond must have been a kettle-hole bog that was gradually closing in from the sides with much of the pond edge floating (as in quaking bogs). When the water level was raised, a portion of this floating root mass broke free and floated to the surface, where it still floats.

The floating island on Sadawga has at times been a headache to the lakeside residents on the northern and eastern shoreline. In 1926 a large section of the island broke off in a storm and for several years proceeded to float around the pond, periodically lodging in front of cottages and disrupting access to the water. That has continued to happen from time to time, though rarely. The main island is probably becoming

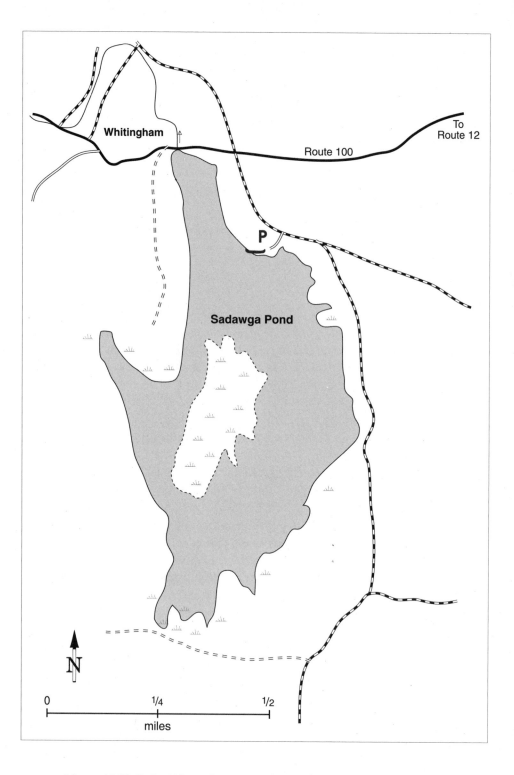

Whitingham

To Route 12

Route 100

P

Sadawga Pond

N

0   1/4   1/2

miles

ever-more solidly anchored to the ground beneath the pond. The name Sadawga derives either from the Mohawk Indian word meaning "swiftly flowing water," or, according to local lore, from an old Indian by that name who stayed in the area long after his people left. Given the stillness of the pond, I tend to believe the latter explanation.

GETTING THERE: The state fishing access at the northern end is on an unmarked paved road that turns south off Route 100 just east of the town of Whitingham. If you're coming via Route 100 from the east, this road is 3.3 miles from the intersection with Route 12. The fishing access is about 0.2 mile from Route 100.

Except for the northern and eastern ends, Sadawga is relatively undeveloped, and the houses unobtrusive. There are extensive marshy areas along the shoreline and a few shallow inlets to explore. Much of the shoreline, like the floating island, is fenlike, with sweetgale, cranberry, various heaths, and the diminutive sundew growing on tussocks of sphagnum moss and grass.

I saw lots of wood ducks here, as well as a rather large gathering of Canada geese, in mid-September. Farther away from the water the land is heavily wooded, with such species as red maple, hemlock, and beech. I also noticed a few large shad or serviceberry trees growing along the shore, some with trunks as large as eight inches in diameter. Fish found here include horned pout, pickerel, yellow perch, and largemouth bass.

I don't recommend getting out of your canoe and walking on the island. While it's tempting to feel a floating sphagnum mat underfoot, your footsteps could impart considerable damage to the fragile fen ecosystem. And it could be dangerous if you fell through the cushiony mat into the water below, which at places is quite deep.

Camping is not permitted at Sadawga Pond, and there are no private campgrounds in the immediate area. Green Mountain National Forest, however, is not too far to the north and west, and offers primitive camping opportunities. For a map and information on primitive camping, write to the Manchester Ranger District, Green Mountain National Forest, RR1, Box 1940, Manchester Center, VT 05255; 802-362-2307.

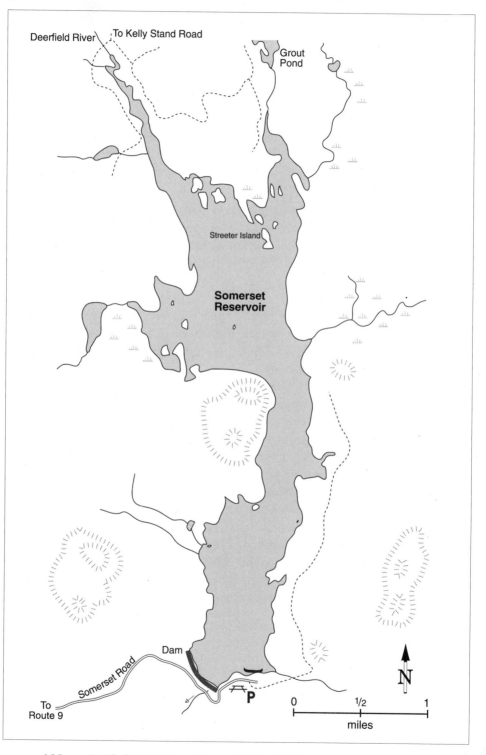

Deerfield River
To Kelly Stand Road

Grout
Pond

Streeter Island

**Somerset
Reservoir**

Dam

Somerset Road

To
Route 9

P

N

0   1/2   1
miles

Somerset Reservoir

Somerset, VT

For the paddler looking for some real exercise in beautiful surroundings, a day on Somerset Reservoir could be just the thing. This long, narrow 1,600-acre lake on the upper reaches of the Deerfield River in southern Vermont is bounded by rolling mountains, including Mount Snow, the northern face of which is visible from most of the lake. Though surrounded by Green Mountain National Forest, the lake itself is owned and managed by the New England Power Company (NEPCO), which prohibits camping or overnight parking at the primary access point at the southern end.

The lake extends roughly five miles from the dam at the southern end to the farthest canoeable point at the northern end where the East Branch of the Deerfield River flows in. Another arm extends farther to the east, fed by a creek coming out of Grout Pond. The northern portion of the lake has a number of nice islands, including Streeter Island, which is maintained as a picnic area by NEPCO. To explore the whole sixteen-mile perimeter would require a full day. If you tend to stop frequently to enjoy the wildlife, as I do—I watched a mink drag a pumpkinseed sunfish, which was almost as large as the mink, along the western shore near the northern end of the lake—you may have trouble getting all the way around in a day. The heavily wooded shoreline lends itself well to relaxed exploring and wildlife observation. The mixed deciduous and conifer woods are full of warblers, woodpeckers, and other birds.

The level of Somerset Reservoir is controlled by NEPCO, with water used for hydropower generation (the water flows into a penstock at Searsburg Dam, which you pass driving into Somerset from Route 9). High-water level is maintained through the loon nesting season (May through July)—Somerset is the southernmost Vermont lake with nesting loons—but after July the level can drop significantly, making the reservoir less attractive to the paddler.

GETTING THERE: To reach Somerset, turn north off Route 9 onto Somerset Road about six miles west of Wilmington. There is a sign at the turnoff for a NEPCO picnic area, but no sign for the lake itself (which is fine with me). This gravel road takes you roughly nine miles north to a parking and picnic area near the dam at the southern end of the lake. There is a boat ramp at this point, and you're likely to see boat trailers parked in the lot. There are outhouses at the picnic area.

Another way to reach the lake is to portage in from the north. You can carry down a logging road off Kelly Stand Road (also known as West Wardsboro-Arlington Road) just to the west of the access road to Grout Pond (see page 103), or carry in from the Grout Pond Recreation Area on marked trails. From the Grout Pond Recreation Area, the carry into the northern end of Somerset is about 0.8 mile.

Contact Green Mountain National Forest to obtain maps of the trails and logging roads in this area (Manchester Ranger District, GMNF, RR 1, Box 1940, Manchester Center, VT 05255; 802-362-2307). While camping is not permitted on the land immediately surrounding Somerset, primitive camping is permitted on the National Forest land. Contact the District Ranger Office for a map that delineates the National Forest boundaries.

Grout Pond
Stratton, VT

Grout Pond is one of the spots our family returns to year after year. Though small (86 acres), the lake offers plenty of space for a relaxed day of canoeing, without the distraction of loud motorboats or water-skiers. Grout Pond is located in Green Mountain National Forest, a large (292,000 acres) federally owned forest in the southern half of Vermont. There are two shelters on the northeastern shore and a half-dozen other tent sites with fireplaces and picnic tables scattered around the lake. Near the entrance to the recreation area is a larger cabin with room for more than a dozen campers. You have to carry your canoe about fifty yards from the parking area to get to the launching area, but it's an easy portage. We generally pile all our camping gear into the canoe and paddle across the lake looking for a nice camping spot (depending on how much gear we've brought, and whether we have our dog with us, a couple of family members usually have to hike around the lake, instead of boating over).

Grout Pond is an ideal spot to acquaint young children with canoe camping. With a trail all the way around the lake and a quick paddle from even the farthest campsite, you're never very far away from your car and civilization. Yet the camping is primitive and much different from what you will find at public or private campgrounds with close-together campsites, RVs, and the like. Kids will enjoy the sandy swimming beach at the northern access point, and there are plenty of places to fish for yellow perch, sunfish, and bass (though fish are small here, due perhaps to the pond's low pH from acid rain). You can be pretty certain of seeing beaver if you paddle on the lake in the late evening or early morning—this is where our daughters got their first good look at these industrious animals (see page 108 for interesting facts about beaver).

As in most of Green Mountain National Forest, primitive camping is permitted anywhere in this area. For information on primitive camping with minimum impact on the environment, see the excellent book *Soft Paths*, (Stackpole Books, 1988).

We often come to Grout Pond in the autumn for our last camping trip of the year. The lake is gorgeous in its full autumn regalia of reds and yellows, especially against a brilliant blue autumn sky (which by this time is free of bugs). Some of the red maples growing along the shore are simply breathtaking.

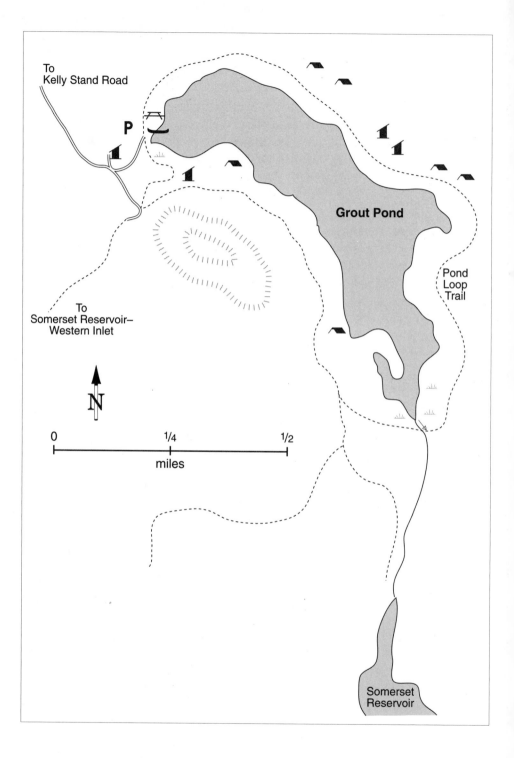

To
Kelly Stand Road

P

Grout Pond

Pond
Loop
Trail

To
Somerset Reservoir–
Western Inlet

N

0   1/4   1/2

miles

Somerset
Reservoir

GETTING THERE: You can reach Grout Pond from either the east or west, off Kelly Stand Road (sometimes called West Wardsboro-Arlington Road), which is a well-maintained gravel road (from Grout Pond west, the road is not plowed in the winter). Most visitors will turn onto Kelly Stand Road from Route 100 in West Wardsboro, approximately 14 miles north of Route 9, or 9 miles south of Route 30. Turn west on Kelly Stand Road toward the town of Stratton. The turnoff to the lake is about 6 miles from West Wardsboro. The road down to Grout Pond is well-marked and 1.0 mile long.

There are numerous trails in the area, including one that extends around the lake and one that leads down to the northern end of Somerset Reservoir. For a trail map of the area, contact the Manchester Ranger District, Green Mountain National Forest, RR 1, Box 1940, Manchester Center, VT 05255; 802-362-2307.

An early morning paddle on Grout Pond, with the mist still rising from the quiet water.

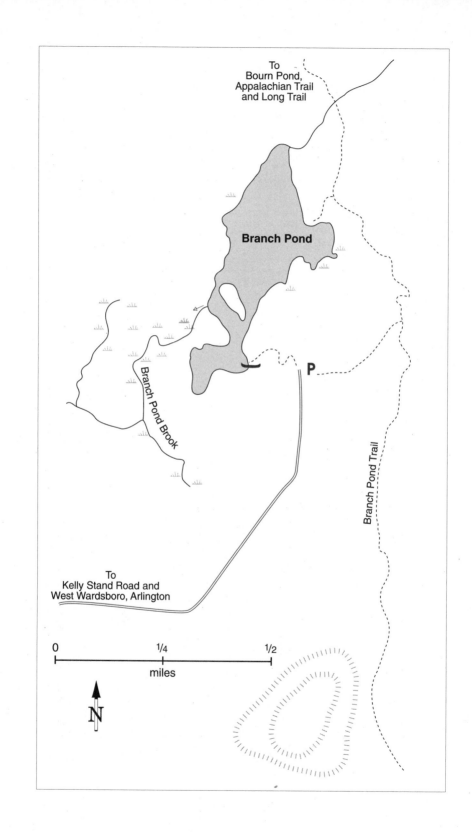

To
Bourn Pond,
Appalachian Trail
and Long Trail

Branch Pond

Branch Pond Brook

P

Branch Pond Trail

To
Kelly Stand Road and
West Wardsboro, Arlington

0   1/4   1/2
miles

N

Branch Pond

Sunderland, VT

Nestled high in the Lye Brook Wilderness of Green Mountain National Forest sits Branch Pond. As lakes go, it is tiny—not even forty acres—but it's a real gem and worthy of inclusion here for its pristine beauty and unusual vegetation. It offers a wonderful morning or afternoon of leisurely paddling. Branch Pond is a fen, and you can find many unusual plants here, including the carnivorous sundew and pitcher plant growing on tussocks of sphagnum moss. Along the shore you'll see a few tamarack or larch trees, a northern species that is our only conifer to lose its needles in the winter. The water is clear and the varied shoreline offers opportunity for some exploring, though access may be somewhat restricted by lake vegetation. Be very careful walking on the sphagnum moss tussocks; your footsteps can damage the fragile plants.

GETTING THERE: To get into Branch Pond, take Kelly Stand Road (sometimes called West Wardsboro-Arlington Road) from either West Wardsboro or Arlington. If you're coming from West Wardsboro (off Route 100), drive west for approximately 11 miles and turn right onto a well-marked gravel road indicating Branch Pond. Proceed 2.5 miles to the end, where you can park. From here, you need to carry down to Branch Pond (approximately 0.3 mile). It is an easy portage to the put-in point, with the trail leading through deep spruce-fir woods full of trillium and lots of other spring wildflowers. For hikers, another trail leads to Bourn Pond and Stratton Pond farther north—both of which have camping shelters—and to an intersection with the Appalachian Trail and Long Trail.

Grout Pond and the northern trail access to Somerset Reservoir are just twenty minutes away by car, reachable by driving back to Kelly Stand Road, then east for about 4.5 miles and south to Grout Pond (see sections on Grout Pond and Somerset Reservoir).

There are several primitive campsites around Branch Pond, and camping is permitted anywhere in this part of Green Mountain National Forest. The ecosystem around Branch Pond is quite fragile, however, so be very careful when camping (see the excellent book *Soft Paths*, published by Stackpole Books, for specifics on low-impact camping). There are outhouses at the parking area by the Branch Pond access.

The Beaver
Wetlands Engineer

The beaver, *Castor canadensis,* is one of the most fascinating and remarkable animals found in our lakes, ponds, and streams. Unlike almost any other animal except human beings, beavers actively modify their environment. This thirty- to sixty-pound beast—the largest rodent in North America—is the sole representative of the family Castoridae, and directly descended from a bear-sized ancestor that lived a million years ago.

Beaver dams and lodges are a familiar site to any paddler who spends much time on New England's lakes and ponds. Both are constructed primarily from branches, placed one by one by the industrious beavers, working mostly under the cover of darkness. (Before Europeans came to America and nearly wiped them out, beavers worked by day and slept at night, but their habits changed to improve chances of survival as early settlers sought their fine pelts.)

A beaver dam is built to raise the level of water in a stream or pond, providing the resident beavers with access to trees growing farther away. The deeper water also allows beavers to reach branches that they have stored underwater, even when the pond is frozen. Beaver dams can be very large, over ten feet high and hundreds of feet long. The largest dam ever recorded, which spanned 4,000 feet and created a lake with forty beaver lodges, was near the present town of Berlin, New Hampshire.

Beavers aren't the only ones to benefit from the dams. Their ponds provide important habitat for waterfowl, fish, and other animals. The dams provide flood control, minimize erosion along stream banks, increase aquifer recharge, and improve water quality both by reducing silting of streams and by providing habitat for marsh plants that help purify water. Beavers are credited with creating much of America's best farmland by damming watercourses and allowing nutrient-rich silt to accumulate.

The lodges constructed by beavers include an underwater entrance and usually two different platform levels: a main floor about four inches above the water level, and a sleeping shelf another two inches higher. The lodge may be constructed in the center of a pond, totally surrounded by water, but more common is a lodge built into the edge of the pond or lake. Before the onset of winter, beavers cover much of the lodge with mud that freezes to provide an almost impenetrable fortress. (Otters are the only predator that can get in, by swimming through the underwater

entrance.) The peak is left more permeable for ventilation.

Near the lodge, in the deep water, beavers store up a winter's worth of branches in an underwater food cache. The branches are stuck butt-first in the mud at the bottom of the pond to keep them under the ice. In the dead of winter beavers swim out of their lodges under the ice and bring back branches to eat. During the spring and summer months, beavers eat primarily pond vegetation, shrubs, herbaceous plants along the shore, and even algae.

Beavers are remarkably well adapted to their unique lifestyle. They have two layers of fur: long, silky guard hairs and a dense, wooly underfur. By regularly grooming this fur with a special comblike split toenail and keeping it oiled, water seldom reaches the beaver's skin. The ears and nose have special valves that allow them to be totally stoppered shut when underwater, and special folds of skin in the mouth enable the beaver to gnaw branches underwater and carry them in its teeth without getting water in its mouth. The back feet have fully webbed toes to provide propulsion underwater, and the tail provides important rudder control, which helps the beaver swim in a straight line when dragging a large branch. Both the respiratory and circulatory systems are adapted to underwater swimming and enable a beaver to stay underwater for up to 15 minutes, during which time it can swim a half mile. Finally, a beaver's teeth are constantly growing and being sharpened through use.

Castor oil, that medicinal cure-all of yesteryear, comes from special perineal scent glands on the beaver. The oily yellow liquid, called castoreum, is used by beavers in waterproofing their fur and in communicating. Along the banks of ponds and lakes where beavers live, you may see mud mounds scented with castoreum that serve in marking territory or communicating in other, less understood ways. The castoreum has a strong but not unpleasant smell and is used as the base ingredient in some expensive perfumes.

Beavers generally mate for life and maintain an extended family structure. Beaver young stay with their parents for two years, so both yearlings and the current year's kits will live with the two parents in the lodge. Two or sometimes three kits are born between April and June. Their eyes are open, they are fully furred, and can walk and swim almost right away, though they rarely leave the lodge until they are at least a month old. The yearlings and both parents bring food to the kits as well as keep up with dam and lodge construction.

The demand for beaver pelts, more than any other factor, was responsible for the early exploration of North America. Beavers were almost exterminated by trappers in the late 1800s, but last-minute legislative protection in the 1890s saved them from extinction. Today, beaver numbers are increasing rapidly, because trapping is less profitable and because most of their natural predators, including wolves, cougars, and bobcats, have been killed off. In fact, beavers are becoming problems in some areas where their engineering activities conflict with those of humans.

As you paddle along the shoreline of lakes or inlet rivers, keep an eye out for tell-tale signs of beavers, including the distinctive stumps left from cut trees or saplings, and well-worn paths leading away from the water's edge where beavers have dragged more distant branches to the water. Beavers are best seen in the late evening or early morning. Paddle up quietly close to a beaver lodge around dusk. If you're patient, you will likely see the animals emerge for evening feeding and perhaps construction work on a dam or lodge. When a beaver senses dan-ger it will slap its tail on the water and dive with a loud *ker-thunk!*

Exploring a quiet beaver pond by canoe—dragging the canoe up over the dam if necessary—can be very rewarding; the pristine pond and marsh provide an ideal habitat for all sorts of wildlife. There are many thousands of beaver dams in New Hampshire and Vermont, some on the inlet streams feeding the lakes and ponds covered in this book, but many more to be found scattered through our region. Some of these won't even show up on topographic maps because they are too small or too recent.

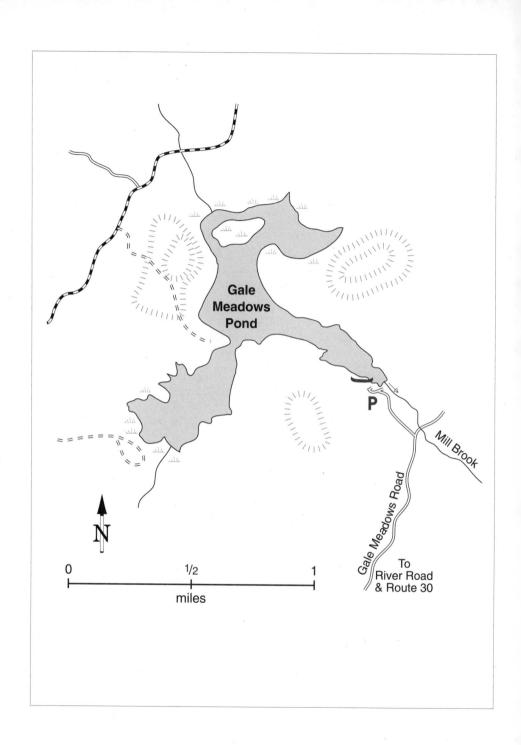

**Gale
Meadows
Pond**

Mill Brook

P

Gale Meadows Road

To
River Road
& Route 30

N

0   1/2   1
miles

Gale Meadows Pond
Winhall, VT

I lived within an hour's drive of Gale Meadows Pond for more than ten years before discovering this out-of-the-way gem. Located just north of Bondville, the 210-acre pond is an ideal spot for a relaxing day of fishing, birdwatching, or simply exploring.

Gale Meadows Pond is shallow with quite a varied shoreline. Parts of the shore, particularly at the southern end, are very marshy. Reeds, sedges, alders, and cattails provide ideal habitat for beaver at this end, and you'll see lots of evidence of them. On the banks are large stands of ferns: ostrich, sensitive, cinnamon, and royal. At both the southern and northern ends the sun-whitened stumps left over from when the pond was dammed provide nesting holes for hundreds of tree swallows, and there are several wood-duck nesting boxes. Pond vegetation and submerged logs may impede paddling in these parts.

The northern end seems much more fenlike, with tamarack and floating sphagnum islands. Except for the swampy areas, most of the shoreline is heavily wooded with mixed conifer and deciduous forest.

Looking northwest across Gale Meadows Pond, with the Bromley ski area in the distance.

There is one farmhouse on the western shore and another house set back from the water at the southern tip, but no recent development. The pond and surrounding area was protected in the early 1960s by a group of area landowners and is managed by the Vermont Department of Fish and Wildlife. In late 1991, a 5 MPH speed limit on Gale Meadows Pond was approved by the Vermont Water Resources Board. This speed limit will make the pond even better for quiet water paddling and fishing. The pond is fished for brown trout, yellow perch, largemouth bass, and horned pout.

GETTING THERE: To reach the pond, take River Road north from Bondville, off Route 30. Coming from the east, River Road cuts back sharply to the right and is paved for the first few hundred feet. After 0.8 mile take a left fork onto Gale Meadows Road. Follow this road for 0.9 mile and take another left fork just before the bridge over Mill Brook. This road dead-ends at the pond's parking and boat launch area.

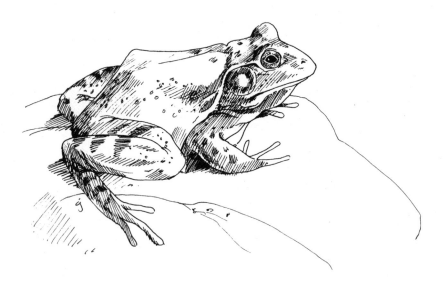

Wallingford Pond

Wallingford, VT

Wallingford Pond is about as remote a body of water as you will find in Vermont. Situated completely within Green Mountain National Forest, the pond is accessible only by foot or by four-wheel-drive with high ground clearance. There is no development on the pond, and about the only sign of people is the road in (which can be pretty chewed up from four-wheel drive trucks), and five or six unmaintained primitive campsites around the pond. Although Wallingford Pond is quite small (86 acres), it seems much larger to me, probably because of its clover-leaf shape, which divides the pond into three segments.

The shoreline is heavily wooded with such species as balsam fir, spruce, red maple, white birch, and yellow birch. Most of the shoreline is quite thickly grown with alders, making access to the shore difficult. Several marshy areas, especially at the inlet near the southern end—provide nesting and feeding habitat for waterfowl and, I'm sure, an occasional moose. Other sections of shoreline seem more boglike, with sphagnum tussocks, heaths, and sundews.

As you paddle into the southern arm of the pond, be careful of sharp rocks just below the surface in the connecting channel. Especially in late summer, when the water level is lower than normal, you need to be careful to avoid damaging your boat.

GETTING THERE: To reach Wallingford Pond from the east or south, drive up Route 103 and turn onto 140 West. Follow the signs for Route 140 West carefully here; you'll make several turns and pass Route 155 almost right away. Route 140 dips down a hill and then up, crossing railroad tracks. Almost immediately after the railroad tracks, take a relatively sharp left onto Sugar Hill Road (this is only about a third of a mile from Route 103). Continue on Sugar Hill Road, which turns to dirt, for 2.4 miles, and turn left onto Wallingford Pond Road (Forest Road 20). Take this road about two miles until you get to a sign for the Wallingford Pond access. There is a parking area for Wallingford Pond, 0.2 mile before the access road to the pond.

If you're coming from the west on Route 140, turn right at the sign for White Rocks Picnic Area, but stay on the main gravel road instead of turning into the picnic area. Go approximately two miles and turn right onto Wallingford Pond Road. Follow directions as above.

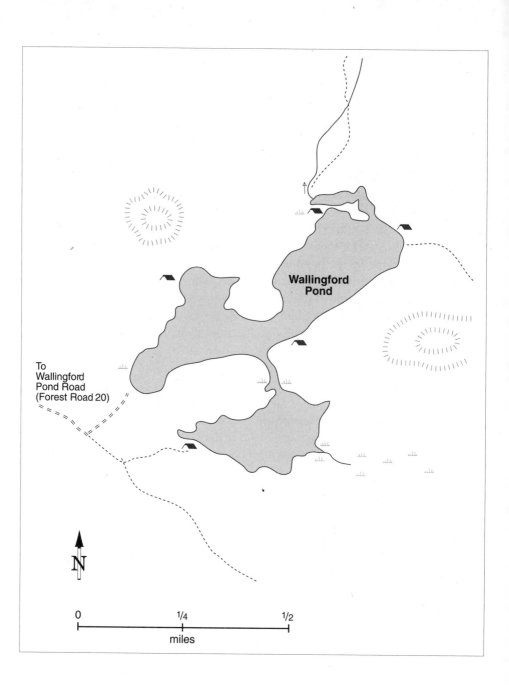

**Wallingford
Pond**

To
Wallingford
Pond Road
(Forest Road 20)

N

| 0 | 1/4 | 1/2 |

miles

Half-submerged rocks guard the channel between Wallingford Pond and its southern branch.

From the Wallingford Pond access sign, you can either attempt to drive in—not recommended unless you have a four-wheel drive vehicle with high ground clearance—or you can carry in. (I feel that to protect the area around the pond and reduce litter, this road *should* be limited to foot travel only.) It took me about thirty minutes to hike in with my canoe. There is a gradual climb, followed by a gradual drop to the pond.

Primitive camping is permitted at the pond. For maps of Green Mountain National Forest and information on trails in the area, contact the Manchester Ranger District, Green Mountain National Forest, RR 1, Box 1940, Manchester Center, VT 05255; 802-362-2307.

Knapp Brook Ponds
Cavendish, VT

The two Knapp Brook Ponds are small but great for a family canoe outing. Other than the state fishing accesses, there is no development on either pond. Pond #1, the first one you reach driving in from the southeast, is smaller (30 acres) and somewhat less interesting. Though there are a couple of islands, the pond is basically round and the shoreline fairly uniform.

Knapp Brook Pond #2 is larger (42 acres) and more fun to explore. It extends to the north, getting you out-of-sight of the fishing access and dam, and there are four or five beaver lodges along the shoreline. You will see a few marshy areas along the edge of the pond, with sedges, reeds, and a few cattails, but there are few real inlets or deep coves here. There is an island that would make a great picnic area—there's even a fire ring to heat some water for tea on a cool autumn morning.

The shorelines of both ponds are heavily wooded: yellow birch, red oak, beech, red spruce, balsam fir, and white pine. Understory shrubs include the large-leaf hobblebush (a viburnum) and alder. Rolling wooded hills surround the ponds.

GETTING THERE: To reach the Knapp Brook Ponds, take Route 131 West from I-91 (Exit 8). Drive 6.9 miles and turn right onto Route 106 North. Go 3.4 miles on Route 106, and turn left onto an unmarked paved road. Stay on this road 1.4 miles; it turns to dirt after about a mile. Turn right onto Knapp Pond Road (this is a shallow right; a smaller road goes off at a sharp right). You will reach the state fishing access for Knapp Brook Pond #1 about a mile down this road; the access for Pond #2 is about a quarter-mile farther.

If you're coming from the west, take Route 103 South from Ludlow and then Route 131 East toward Cavendish. Drive about six miles on Route 131 and watch for Tarbell Hill Road (paved) to the left. You will see a sign for Caton Place Campground. Turn here and drive 3.0 miles, staying on the paved road, then turn left onto Knapp Pond Road. You can park at either pond. If you want to paddle on both, it's an easy portage between them at the connecting creek (about 60 yards) over a wide grassy area.

There is no camping at the Knapp Brook Ponds, but there is a private campground a few miles away off Tarbell Hill Road (I have not

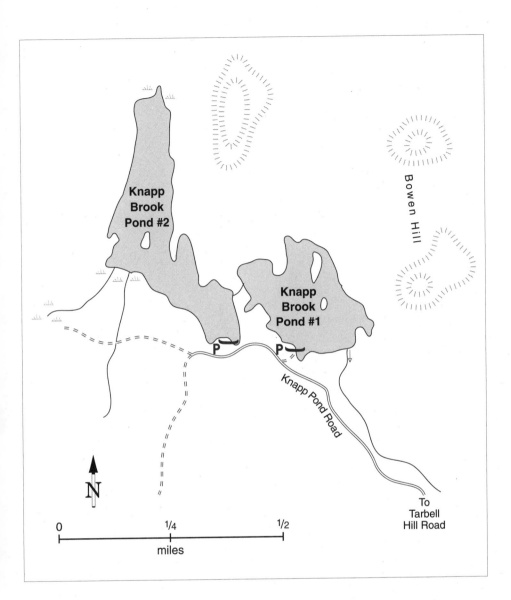

camped here). For information, contact Caton Place Campground, Cavendish, VT 05142; 802-226-7767. There are supposed to be some trails in the 1,000-acre Wildlife Management Area surrounding the Knapp Brook Ponds, but the only trail I could find (which went generally north from the dam at Pond #1) tapered out fairly quickly. Though small, the Knapp Brook Ponds can provide an enjoyable morning or afternoon of paddling for a family, with a chance to see turtles, beaver, and great blue herons, and fish for rainbow and brook trout.

Central Vermont

Lake Champlain: Southern End
West Haven, Benson, VT

Most of Lake Champlain is too large to tackle in an open canoe, but the southern end can be an enjoyable exception. (I say "can be" because even here, wind sometimes produces dangerous paddling conditions, and the wakes from large boats can swamp a canoe.) Near the southern tip of the lake, about a mile north of where the Poultney River flows in, is a canoe access point on the Bald Mountain Nature Conservancy property.

GETTING THERE: This access is a little difficult to get to. You really need detailed road maps or topographic maps of both the Vermont and New York sides. The access road skirts the southern edge of the nub of Vermont that dips into New York, along the Poultney River. Cross over the Poultney River into Vermont as far south in this little southern extension as possible, then turn left (west) and follow a poorly maintained dirt road along the river for about 1.5 miles. A marked canoe access is on the left, with limited parking for four or five cars about 50 yards back down the road on the other side. A number of other access points farther north along the lake are mentioned below.

The extreme southern tip of Lake Champlain up to Benson Landing is very narrow. The banks are marshy, with silver maples and old willows reaching their branches out over the fairly murky water. A railroad follows the west bank of the river (New York side), but otherwise there is little development visible from the water. You're likely to see great blue herons, lots of tree swallows, and numerous songbirds in the trees along the shore. Painted turtles will slide into the water from partially submerged logs as you pass by. There are numerous backwaters and inlets to explore along this section of lake that are thick with

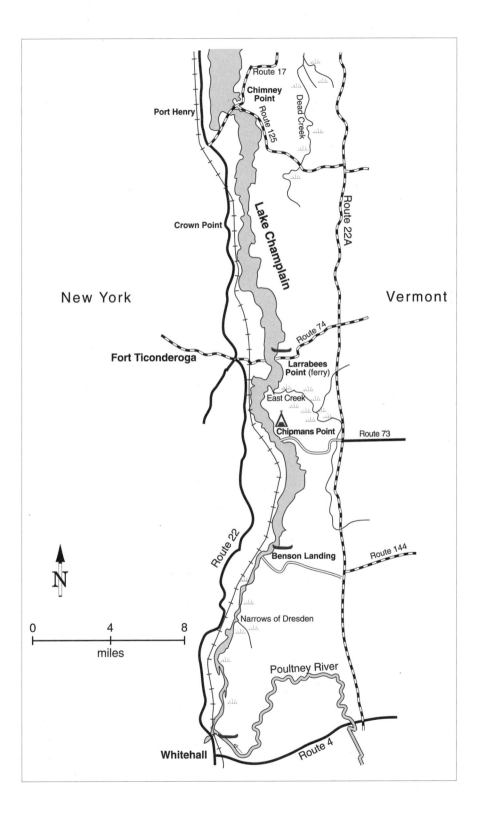

vegetation, including cattails, sedges, arrowhead, and, unfortunately, Eurasian milfoil, an introduced aquatic plant that is choking out other plants in lakes where it has become established.

Halfway up to Benson Landing, you will pass through the Narrows of Dresden, a beautiful section of lake bounded by tall cliffs with cedar, hemlock, and white birch growing out of crevices in the rock and hanging down to the water's edge. Though the narrowness of the lake here seems comforting, be careful of the wakes made by larger boats. Large cabin cruisers pass through on the way from the Great Lakes to Florida, via the New York Barge Canal (which extends south from the Poultney River). A forty-foot cabin cruiser, as we found out, creates a very large wake. In a lake only one or two hundred yards wide, you will get the full impact, which can be a three-foot wave—enough to swamp an open canoe if you don't deal with it just right. In most cases, it's best to point the canoe into an approaching wave, but escaping into a protected cove or behind an island, when possible, is better. We found ourselves constantly looking over our shoulders and planning a route of escape. Be very careful.

If you're just out for the day, or if it's windy, you may want to turn around where the lake opens up about a mile south of Benson Landing. If you are continuing, be aware that from this point north you're getting into big water, where the lake is a mile wide in many stretches. There is a good boat access at Benson Landing, with parking for at least a dozen cars, and a smaller landing three miles up, in the town of Orwell. Along this section of the lake with a moderate wind (ten to fifteen knots) out of the north, we experienced waves a foot and a half high, some of which lapped over the bow of our heavily-laden canoe. There are some fairly remote stretches of shoreline along here that are suitable for camping, or you can continue north to Chipman's Point, where camping is available at the Chipman Point Marina (RR 1, Box 90, Orwell, VT 05760; 802-948-2288).

A fantastic side trip can be made on East Creek, which flows into the lake across from Fort Ticonderoga. You can paddle four or five miles up this meandering brook through cattail and sedge marshes and along deep deciduous woods and grassy dairy fields. Bring along a fishing rod if you're interested in some fine bass fishing. You'll pass shagbark hickory trees, white oaks, and basswood along with the more typical Vermont tree species. The variety of habitats found along East Creek provide some excellent birdwatching. Unfortunately, you cannot canoe all the way in on East Creek to a road access—your way is eventually blocked by a large, beautiful falls over a steeply sloping rock face—but you can reach a road on the North Fork of East Creek, though it will be a bit of a struggle carrying over several beaver dams. Along the North Branch are

Loading up the canoe at the narrow south end of Lake Champlain. The bicycle is for a return trip to the car.

some of the largest silver maple trees I've ever seen. The one we had lunch under looked at least twenty-four feet in circumference! (Note that this is all private farmland through here—be respectful.)

Back out on Lake Champlain, it is a relatively short paddle from the East Creek inlet to Larrabees Point, where a ferry crosses over to New York. From Larrabees Point north the lake gradually widens, but is still canoeable up to the bridge at Chimney Point, another fourteen miles or so above Larrabees Point. From that point north, the lake is just too big to be enjoyable to the open-boat paddler (see the section on the Missisquoi River Delta, which is at the far northern end of the lake).

The adventurous might want to try what a friend and I did on this section of the lake. We took a bicycle along in the canoe, and after two days of canoeing, the guy with the short straw got to bicycle back to the car (the New York side is a little more direct, via Route 22) and drive back to pick up the canoe and the well-rested canoeing partner. This way, you don't need two cars.

A trip on Lake Champlain, even on the more manageable southern section, takes more planning than most of the other trips covered in this book. For more detailed information, get hold of USGS topographic maps or the *Vermont Atlas and Gazetteer* (DeLorme Mapping Company).

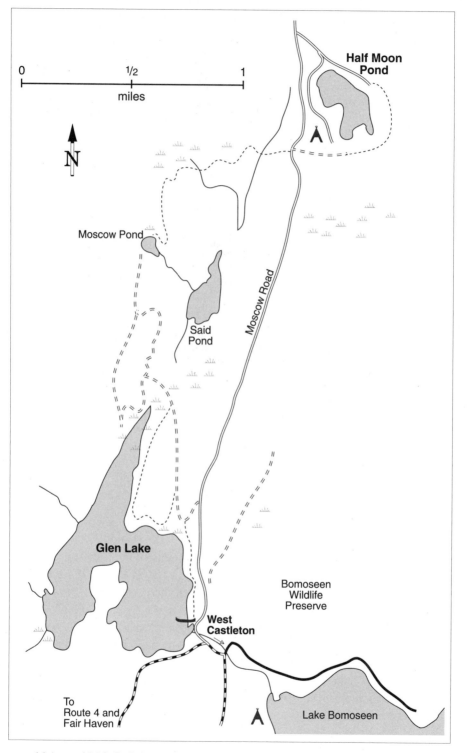

Glen Lake and Half Moon Pond
Castleton, VT

Glen Lake is located in western Vermont, at the northern reaches of the Taconic Mountains. There are a number of slate quarries nearby, some of which still produce the slate shingles Vermont is known for. You can get a real feel for the sedimentary geology at Glen Lake by paddling around the shoreline, which is mostly exposed ledge of this layered rock. Millions of years ago, clays accumulated at the bottom of the ocean and were compressed into shale. When that ocean floor was uplifted into the Taconic Mountains, heat and pressure metamorphosed the shale into much harder slate.

Canoeing is very pleasant here. A five-mile-per-hour speed limit for motorboats keeps most large boats away. The midsize lake (about 200 acres) has only minimal development on it. At the southern end near the dam and put-in point are three or four houses. The rest of the shore is mostly wild and heavily wooded (principally hemlock, white pine, red maple, and white birch). From the outlet, the Glen Lake trail extends around the eastern shoreline on public land. The trail rounds the northern tip of Glen Lake, then extends up to Moscow Pond and Half Moon Pond. Though not readily accessible by trail, with a topographical map you should be able to find Said Pond, southwest of Moscow Pond. (You can get a map of this and other trails at Half Moon State Park or Bomoseen State Park, just southeast of Glen Lake.) Another trail, the Slate History Trail, takes you through what is left of the West Castleton Railroad and Slate Company. A self-guiding pamphlet describes the area's slate history. Ask for this information at either of the park offices.

Although camping is not permitted on Glen Lake, you can camp at Half Moon Pond, which is 2.8 miles north on Moscow Road (dirt). Half Moon Pond State Park is a very pleasant campground, and the pond offers some enjoyable paddling, although it is a little too small for the use it receives from over sixty campsites and lean-tos around the pond. There's a beaver lodge at the northern end, which you might want to check out in the evening or early morning, when beaver are most active. Canoes can be rented at Half Moon Pond State Park.

GETTING THERE: To get to Glen Lake from the south, take the paved road that leads north from Fair Haven to West Castleton (from the east, get off Route 4 at Exit 3 and turn north onto this road). You will see the access to Glen Lake 4.3 miles north of Route 4 (coming up

This stately white pine clings to the rocky shoreline of Glen Lake, in the heart of Vermont's slate country.

from Fair Haven, you will cross over Route 4). From the north, take Moscow Road south 2.8 miles past Half Moon Pond, bearing right in West Castleton, and look for the Glen Lake access on the right.

Bring your fishing rod. Rainbow trout are caught here, and I was told that somebody once pulled a thirty-pound northern pike out of Glen Lake.

Chittenden Reservoir and Lefferts Pond
Chittenden, VT

Chittenden Reservoir is a little difficult to find, but the effort is definitely worth it. Motorboats are limited to fifteen horsepower on Chittenden, so you needn't worry about being run over by water-skiers and large watercraft. There are numerous inlets and bays to explore around the lake perimeter, providing a full day (or more) of canoeing. Unfortunately, Central Vermont Public Service Corporation (CVPS), which owns the reservoir, does not permit overnight camping. Water level can fluctuate somewhat from week to week because water is drawn off the lake for power generation. If one of the other power plants providing power to CVPS shuts down, you can expect the water level in Chittenden to drop by as much as four feet.

There are put-in points with day parking at both southern ends of the 674-acre lake and at the southern tip of Lefferts Pond. The western put-in is more developed and suitable for trailered motorboats, while the eastern access points require a carry. Because Chittenden is quite large, winds can be strong on the lake. On a breezy day, stick close to the coves, or paddle on Lefferts Pond.

In early spring Lefferts pond is quite canoeable, but as this stubble of last year's vegetation indicates, the pond becomes much less navigable by early summer.

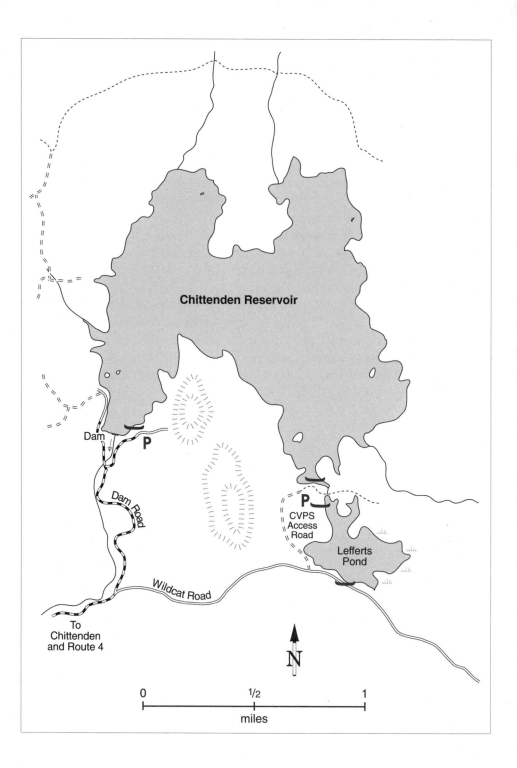

Chittenden Reservoir

Dam

Dam Road

P

CVPS
Access
Road

Lefferts
Pond

Wildcat Road

To
Chittenden
and Route 4

N

0   1/2   1
miles

Lefferts Pond is a real gem. It is small (fifty-five acres) and very shallow, but rich in wildlife. On an April morning not long after ice-out, I watched a river otter pull a six- or seven-inch fish up on a rock and eat it. You can also expect to see beaver, muskrat, and lots of waterfowl, including wood duck, which often nest in boxes CVPS has put up on both Lefferts and Chittenden. A pair of loons also frequently nests on Chittenden or Lefferts, making this one of only a handful of lakes in Vermont that supports nesting loons. (The loons' nesting success depends on people like us keeping our distance during nesting season—see page 51.)

Lefferts Pond and the area immediately surrounding it is a Wildlife Management Area and therefore more protected than Chittenden. No gasoline-powered boats are permitted, and because the pond is shallow, weeds restrict paddling during much of the season on the southern end.

The Chittenden/Lefferts Pond area is nestled into the beautiful Green Mountains of central Vermont. The tall surrounding mountains—some of Vermont's tallest—give the area a wild and remote feeling. Along the shores you'll find mostly hardwood, including several species of both birch and maple, though the hardwoods are interspersed here and there with stands of hemlock, spruce, and balsam fir. On a peak autumn day, this area should be stunning. Plan for a little hiking as well as canoeing. There's a great trail that starts at Lefferts Pond and extends around Chittenden Reservoir. Moss-covered boulders, thick banks of ferns, bubbling brooks, and lots of wildlife provide for great hiking. I saw numerous moose tracks during my visit. If you want to do some hiking, there is access to the famous Vermont Long Trail from here.

Plan your visit to Chittenden Reservoir and Lefferts Pond carefully to avoid the various hunting seasons. The area is very popular with hunters, especially duck hunters, who construct hunting blinds on both Chittenden and Lefferts. For more information, contact Central Vermont Public Service Company, 77 Grove Street, Rutland, VT 05701; 802-773-2711; in Vermont, 800-622-4141. For information on hunting seasons, contact the Vermont Fish and Wildlife Department, 103 South Main St., Waterbury, VT 05676; 802-244-7331.

GETTING THERE: To get to Chittenden Reservoir, drive northeast from Rutland on Route 4 approximately 4.0 miles. In Mendon, turn left toward East Pittsford. At the T, turn right toward Chittenden. Stay to the right where Mountain Top Road bears off to the left, and drive another 2.0 miles, staying on the main road (known locally as Dam

White birch trees reflected in the quiet water of Lefferts Pond on an April morning. Watch for otter here.

Road), and you will reach the boat access at the dam. To reach the eastern carry-in boat launch and Lefferts Pond, bear to the right on Wildcat Road (unpaved) about 1.2 miles after passing the Mountain Top Road turnoff, and then turn left onto an unimproved CVPS access road a little less than a mile from that fork. The gate to this access is open from mid-April (depending on mud conditions) through December. You can also get onto Lefferts Pond by continuing on Wildcat Road past the CVPS access road. You will see the carry-in access on the left as the road passes Lefferts Pond.

Richville Pond

Shoreham, VT

Just to the east of Lake Champlain on the far western side of Vermont lies Richville Pond, another of those winding, marshy bodies of water absolutely brimming with wildlife (see sections on Dead Creek and the southern portion of Lake Champlain, which describes East Creek). Richville Pond can be reached either from Shoreham Center on the north or at the historic Shoreham Covered Bridge on the south.

The pond is a widened section of the Lemon Fair River. At most points it is less than one hundred yards wide. East of the covered bridge, the pond narrows to just a winding creek, which you can follow as far as weed growth allows; by the end of June, passage is fairly restricted along this section. About a half-mile east of the covered bridge, the creek forks and you can take either channel (the smaller north fork is a little difficult to find). From the northern fishing access to the covered bridge is a little less than two miles, and in the spring

The picturesque Shoreham Covered Bridge over Richville Pond is one of only two covered railroad bridges remaining in Vermont

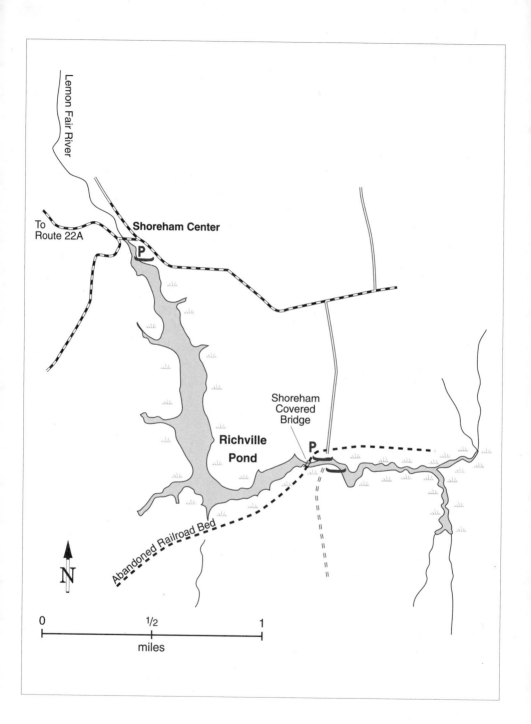

you can paddle at least a mile past the bridge on the narrow creek. The entire shore of the long, narrow pond is marshy and thick with cattails, sedges, bull rushes, arrowhead, wild onion, and white waterlilies. Unfortunately, there is also Eurasian milfoil here, which is choking out some of the native vegetation. Paddling along you will pass through rich, rolling farmland and patchy stands of mixed hardwoods and white pine. The area is alive with songbirds—a birdwatcher's paradise. We watched a whitetail doe grazing in reeds as high as her back and listened to a symphony of songbirds all along the pond. Pickerel fishing is excellent.

The origin of the name "Lemon Fair" has generated quite a bit of disagreement over the years. According to some, it is a corruption of "lamentable affair." In 1824, Zedock Thompson recorded the story that an old woman came across the stream and said it was truly a lamentable affair. Other versions attribute the lamentable affair to an Indian massacre or a drowning. Another explanation is that the name is a transliteration of the French *Les monts Verts* (the green mountains) or, most likely, according to Esther Swift in *Vemont Place Names*, that the name comes from the French name for the river, *Limon Faire* (to make mud).

You will want to spend some time at the Shoreham bridge, which crosses the pond where it narrows toward the eastern end. It is one of just two covered railroad bridges remaining in Vermont. The tall, stately bridge has not been used since 1951, but it is well maintained—quite something for those who have an interest in heavy timber construction.

GETTING THERE: The northern fishing access can be reached by turning east from Route 22A about 0.4 mile south of the intersection of Routes 22A and 74 West. You will see the state fishing access on the right just after crossing the Lemon Fair River (approximately 2.4 miles from Route 22A). To get to the Shoreham Covered Bridge access point, continue past the fishing access and take the first right, onto an unpaved road 3.3 miles from Route 22A. The bridge is 0.7 mile down this road.

There is plenty of parking at the bridge and a well-hidden boat access trail that leads from the parking area down to the water. Most maps show a road crossing the pond just to the east of the covered bridge, but the bridge is closed. Access to either of the maintained parking areas is therefore from the north. If you come in from the south, there is an unmaintained put-in point where the road dead-ends at the closed bridge.

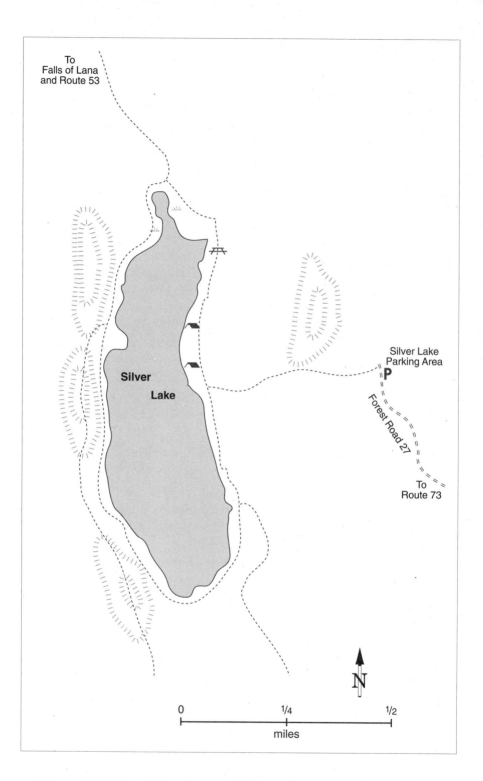

To
Falls of Lana
and Route 53

Silver
Lake

Silver Lake
Parking Area
P

Forest Road 27

To
Route 73

N

0   1/4   1/2

miles

Silver Lake

Leicester, VT

This is really a better place for backpackers than for paddlers, as it's quite a haul into the lake. I expect I'll hear from a disgruntled reader or two who saw the lake listed in the book and, without reading the description, figured it was one of those lakes you can drive to. Well, for the hearty paddler who likes the less-traveled areas and doesn't mind a bit of a portage, Silver Lake is great. The lake itself is quite small (103 acres) and the shoreline is fairly regular, with few coves or marshy areas to explore, but camped under the tall hemlocks and gazing across the lake on a quiet autumn morning, the exquisite setting more than makes up for the lake's limitations.

There are fifteen campsites at the Silver Lake Recreation Area, which is in Green Mountain National Forest. Fresh water is available from two wells with hand pumps, and outhouses are located in both the picnic and camping areas. There is no fee to use the campground, and stays are limited to a very generous two weeks. You can camp here year-round, but the water pump handles are removed before risk of freeze-up. Most of the campsites are close to the water, and a few are really stunning, nestled beneath towering hemlock trees on a thick bed of needles and surrounded by huge rock outcroppings.

GETTING THERE: There are two access routes to the lake. From the west, you can park just off Route 53 (5.3 miles north of the intersection with Route 73) and follow the trail past the Falls of Lana to the lake. The hike in from this direction is 1.5 miles, most of it steeply uphill. The trail leads to the northern end of the lake by the dam and picnic area. The campsites are around the lake to the left on the eastern shore.

For carrying a canoe in, a much better access point is from the east side via forest roads. Take Route 73 east from Route 53 for 1.7 miles and turn left (north) onto Forest Road 32. You will see a sign for Silver Lake at the turnoff. After about a half mile, the road turns to the left across a creek and soon turns to dirt. Just under two and a half miles from Route 73 you will turn left onto Forest Road 27 (a sign points toward Silver Lake). Stay on Forest Road 27, bearing to the right at one questionable point, until you reach the Silver Lake parking area and a barricaded smaller road continuing on (4.5 miles from Route 73). The carry into Silver Lake is 0.6 mile from here, most of it gently downhill. When you get to the Silver Lake Loop trail, the campsites are to the right within a few hundred yards.

Apparently there have been problems with cars being broken into at the parking areas on both the east and west access points. If you stay overnight, after you carry your canoe and gear in from the eastern side, it might be advisable to drive back around via Routes 73 and 53 (past the Falls of Lana trail access) to Branbury State Park on Lake Dunmore, where you can park your car safely for a small fee when the park is open. Then walk back up the trail to Silver Lake. Some people use this approach with a wheeled canoe-portaging cart, bringing the canoe and gear in from the east side (downhill) and leaving on the west side (also downhill).

Besides the Silver Lake Loop trail, there are a number of good trails in this part of Green Mountain National Forest. If you didn't hike in via the Falls of Lana, be sure to check it out. General Wool camped here with his troops in 1850, and his party decided such an attractive place needed a better name than Sucker Brook Falls, so they named it Falls of Lana after their leader—*Lana* is Spanish for wool. Other hiking trails in the vicinity of Silver Lake include the Leicester Hollow, Chandler Ridge, and Goshen trails. Write to the Green Mountain National Forest for a map of Silver Lake and Moosalamoo Hiking Trails (USDA Forest Service, Middlebury Ranger District, RD #3, Middlebury, VT 05753; 802-388-4362).

Branbury State Park, about a half-mile north on Route 53 from the Falls of Lana trailhead, offers car camping with canoeing, although you'll share the water with motorboats. Call 802-247-5925.

tained road bears to the left, while a smaller, unmaintained road goes straight. Continue straight here, downhill, and you will reach the lake access in about 0.2 mile. The road is in poor condition, so be careful.

Park wherever you can find a space. Usage can be high on summer weekends, but the reservoir has the surprising capacity to absorb a lot of people without seeming too crowded. If you want to be more alone here, if your schedule permits, visit midweek before Memorial Day or after Labor Day.

Remember, for the sake of everyone who canoes and camps here, respect the privilege. Carry out everything you bring in, bury any human wastes, minimize your impact on the vegetation when you camp (see the book *Soft Paths*, Stackpole Books, 1988), be sure not to disturb nesting loons or other wildlife, and make a special effort to pick up any litter that others have thoughtlessly left behind.

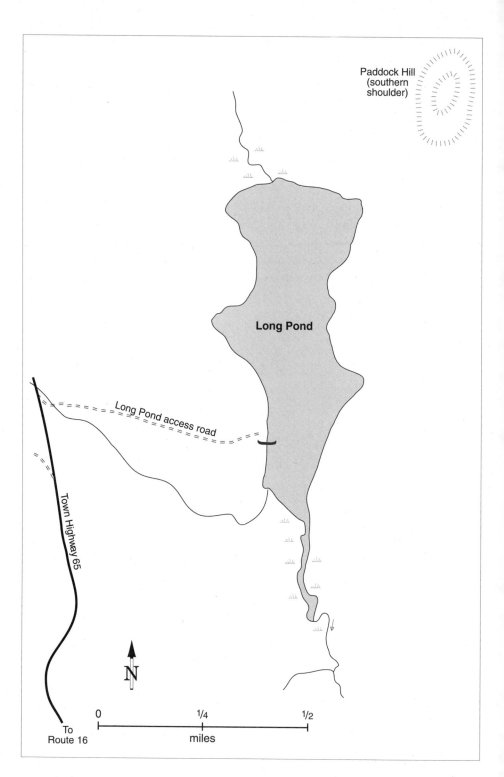

Paddock Hill
(southern
shoulder)

Long Pond

Long Pond access road

Town Highway 65

To
Route 16

N

0	1/4	1/2

miles

Long Pond

Greensboro, VT

Northwest of St. Johnsbury, pretty much in the middle of nowhere in Vermont's Northeast Kingdom, lies Long Pond, one of the state's few undeveloped bodies of water. Gasoline-powered motorboats are prohibited from this pristine 97-acre pond, and the only structure (as of 1991, anyway) is an old cabin on the western side. The Nature Conservancy has protected the southern end of Long Pond as well as 1,500 feet of shoreline on the eastern side.

The vegetation here is typical of lakes in northern Vermont. Northern white cedars line almost the entire perimeter. When northern white cedar is the dominant species along a lake shore, it sometimes looks as if someone trimmed the lower branches to a perfectly horizontal plane—at least when you see the trees from a distance. I had long wondered what controls the height of this horizontal plane and why it occurs. Well, as I recently learned, someone does trim the lower branches: deer. During the winter deer graze on the lower branches from the ice—as far up as they can reach—creating this horizontal plane. Further inland, the cedars give way to balsam fir, hemlock, maple, and other deep-woods species.

There are marshy areas with cattails, floating pond weeds, and various grasses and sedges at both the north inlet and the south outlet. Look for wood duck here. Beavers have a lodge along the western shore, and you're likely to see evidence of their activity, even if you don't see the beavers themselves. Also keep an eye out for otters. I watched one lazily fishing here on a September mid-afternoon. That I saw an otter at midday is testament to the remoteness of this pond; usually, in order to see otter, mink and beaver, you need to get out in the early morning or around dusk.

One reason Long Pond remains so untouched is that it's hard to get to. An unmarked jeep track leads into the pond from Town Highway 65 in Greensboro. Don't even think about driving down this road unless you have a four-wheel drive vehicle with high ground clearance. And even if you have such a vehicle, I suggest parking at the maintained gravel road and carrying in to avoid damage to the grassy area at the pond (especially in wet weather).

GETTING THERE: To get to the access road, the most direct approach is from the southeast off Route 16. From the intersection with Route 15, drive north on Route 16 for 8.5 miles and turn left onto

Taylor Road. From here you will drive 3.7 miles to the Long Pond access road, making a series of alternating lefts and rights onto a number of unmarked or poorly marked roads. From Route 16, bear left after 0.4 mile; bear right after 1.4 miles; bear left after 1.8 miles; and bear right after 2.5 miles. After you've gone 3.7 miles from Route 16, look for a nondescript track on the right that bears off at a sharp angle. If you pass the Long Pond access road, you'll get to Skunk Hollow Road on the right just 0.1 mile farther along.

There is room for several cars to pull over along the gravel road here. The carry to the pond takes about 15 minutes (longer if you take a few rests). The road fords a creek, then rises and falls gently for the half-mile hike to the pond. When you get to the pond there is a nice grassy clearing beneath some large cedars that makes an ideal picnic spot. Camping is not permitted.

Lake Willoughby
Westmore, VT

I debated long and hard whether to include this lake in the guide. It is one of the most beautiful lakes in Vermont, but it is also quite large (1,653 acres), and winds whipping down between the steep cliffs can make canoeing hazardous. Furthermore, the shoreline is fairly uniform, with few if any coves to explore, the northern end is quite developed, there are a lot of motorboats on weekends, and a road runs the entire length of the lake on the eastern shore. All that said, I just couldn't resist including it.

On the southern end, fantastic cliffs of Mount Pisgah to the east and Mount Hor to the west overlook the lake, rising steeply from the lake's shores. Mount Pisgah's cliffs provide some of the best ice climbing in the Northeast, and peregrine falcons have reestablished a nesting site on the cliffs. A trail extends from near the southern end of the lake above the cliffs and over the peak of Mount Pisgah, returning back down to the lake at about its mid-point. On the trail you will see unusual arctic flora, and you may catch a glimpse of the endangered peregrine falcon.

The cliffs of Pisgah Mountain, here viewed from the south, overlook the deep blue waters of Lake Willoughby.

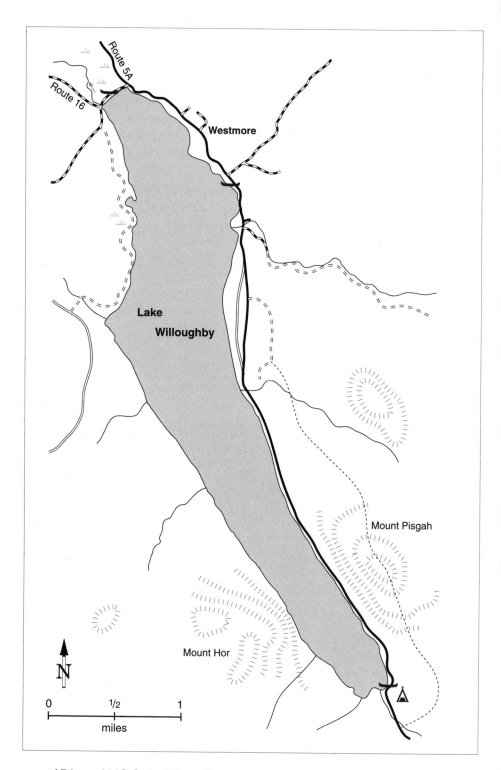

Lake Willoughby is the deepest lake in Vermont, with a maximum depth of 308 feet. Because of the great depth, prize lake trout are taken out of here, including the state record thirty-four-pounder. Lake trout of more than twenty pounds are caught here fairly regularly—though I'm not sure I'd want to fight a twenty-pound fish from a canoe! The lake is also one of the few spots in Vermont where you can catch landlocked salmon.

There are beaches the northern end of Lake Willoughby and another beach and a private campground at the southern end (White Caps Campground, 802-467-3345). If you're paddling the length of the lake, the western shore is somewhat nicer, especially on the southern half of the lake. There are no houses along here, and beautiful northern white cedars sweep down into the lake from their precarious perches on the huge moss- and fern-covered granite boulders, which centuries of erosion have brought down from the cliffs above. Further north, you'll see such species as hemlock, red spruce, and striped maple mixed in with the predominant cedar and birch.

GETTING THERE: You can launch a canoe at the southern end, northern end, or at the state fishing access on the eastern shore off Route 5A, about four-fifths of the way up the lake. Driving south on Route 5A, this fishing access is 1.2 miles from the intersection of Routes 16 and 5A. It is 4.1 miles from the southern end of the lake. If you are driving to Lake Willoughby from the south, take Route 5 North from Lyndonville and I-91, then turn onto Route 5A North in West Burke. You will reach the southern end of the lake approximately six miles from the intersection of Routes 5 and 5A.

Because Lake Willoughby is long and narrow, it's a good lake to paddle just one way (preferably with the wind), if you are able to coordinate a drop off and pick up. Remember, this is a big lake. Winds can come up quickly and create very hazardous paddling conditions. If bad weather threatens, there are plenty of smaller lakes and ponds in the area that will provide quieter, more relaxed paddling (see section on May Pond).

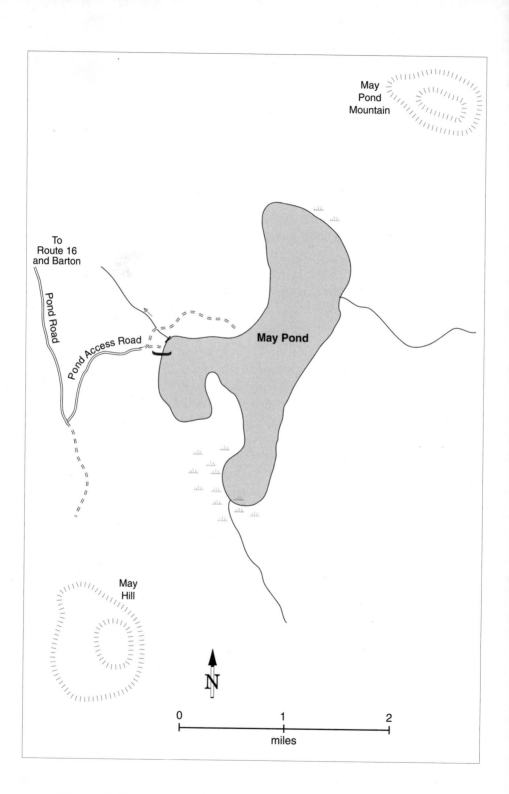

May
Pond
Mountain

To
Route 16
and Barton

Pond Road

Pond Access Road

May Pond

May
Hill

N

0   1   2
miles

May Pond
Barton, VT

Located in Vermont's Northeast Kingdom about a half-hour's drive from Lake Willoughby, this little-known pond is a real gem. Though small (116 acres) the pond is highly varied and seems much larger. It's a great spot for an early morning or late afternoon paddle, when some of the area wildlife is likely to be more active. I watched a family of four otter here for about an hour one August evening around dusk diving for crayfish and eating them at the surface. There are also beaver, nesting loons—at least they successfully nested in 1991—and possibly osprey nesting nearby (I watched one fishing at the pond).

May Pond is quite remote. There are only two cabins here—both relatively close to the dam and state fishing access, and the eastern side of the pond is bordered by rolling farmland. But other than these rather modest signs of civilization, the pond is totally wild. Much of the shoreline is marshy, with lots of pond vegetation (water-shield lilies, cattails, sedges, and the like), and the rest of the shoreline is densely grown with fairly impenetrable shrubs (heaths, winterberry, alders). Farther back on solid ground are red spruce, balsam fir, white and yellow birch, red maple, and hemlock. The shallower southern end of the pond is more fenlike, with tussocks of sphagnum moss, sundews, and the thick muck of decomposing vegetation that your paddle stirs up. In the springtime, you'll see laurel blooming, and in mid-summer you may be able to enjoy a snack of wild blueberries. The southern end is where you'll also find a huge beaver lodge—likely the home of many generations of beaver.

Surrounded by gentle hills and with a real feeling of remoteness, May Pond is one of my favorites. There's no camping here, but there are several private campgrounds in the area, and Brighton State Park (see section on Spectacle Pond) is not too far away. The closest private campground is the Bellview Campground in Barton, just a couple of miles away, overlooking Crystal Lake. I haven't camped here and understand that most sites are for RVs, but you may want to check it out (for information, call 802-525-3242). Brook trout fishing is supposed to be quite good at May Pond.

Recognizing May Pond's pristine ecological character, the Vermont Nature Conservancy has purchased 740 acres around the pond, including five thousand feet of frontage. (For more information on May Pond, write to the Vermont Nature Conservancy, 27 State St., Montpelier, VT 05602; 802-229-4425.) As you paddle around May Pond, respect its fragile character, and be extremely careful not to disturb nesting loons, otter and other wildlife.

GETTING THERE: To get to May Pond from the west (from the town of Barton and Interstate 91, Exit 25), turn off Route 5 onto Route 16 North (which heads more east at this point). Drive 1.6 miles and turn right onto Pond Road, an unmarked dirt road heading southeast. This road forks after 1.4 miles—stay to the right. After driving 2.1 miles from Route 16, turn left into the state fishing access. You'll see the pond about a quarter mile down this road. If you're coming from the east on Route 16, the dirt road leading to the pond is 5.7 miles from the intersection of Routes 16 and 5A at the northern end of Lake Willoughby.

Spectacle Pond
Brighton, VT

Spectacle Pond, next to Island Pond in Vermont's Northeast Kingdom, is a small but quite varied 102-acre pond. It is said that this pond was a stop on the annual travels of the Algonquin Indians and that the distinct point on its eastern shore served as a meeting ground. Visiting the pond and that point of land, one can believe these stories. Though now grown up in a stand of red pine, the area once had towering white pines that provided shade for encampments and meetings. The pond itself is a glacial kettle hole pond, formed thousands of years ago when a chunk of the receding glacier was left buried in the glacial till. The ice gradually melted, leaving behind the shallow basin, which filled to form the pond.

Much of Spectacle Pond is surrounded by Brighton State Park, which has sixty-three tent sites and twenty-one lean-tos, many of them on the water. At the southern end is a swimming beach and boat rentals for campers. Several trails extend around the southeastern end of the pond (maps are available from the park headquarters), and there is a small museum, though its hours of operation are very limited. You might see a moose when hiking the trails in the park. There is a nice children's playground located off the road that connects the campsites. Fishing is popular both here and in nearby Island Pond. In short, it's a great spot for families, with plenty of outdoor activities for everybody.

Brown trout, horned pout, and smallmouth bass are caught in both ponds; rainbow trout and Walleye pike, only in Island Pond. If you aren't camping at Brighton State Park, there is a public boat access on the northwestern corner of Spectacle Pond. The public access to Island Pond is about a mile from Spectacle Pond.

Like much of the Northeast Kingdom, Spectacle Pond's surrounding woodlands are northern boreal forests, dominated by balsam fir, red spruce, northern white cedar, white birch, and red maple. Northern white cedar is also called *arbor vitae*—the tree of life. Historians believe it was named by the French explorer Jacques Cartier, who made a tea from the tree to cure his men of scurvy. You will also see red pine here, probably planted in the 1930s. There are some interesting marshy areas around the pond, including the channel leading from Spectacle into Island Pond (it is not possible to canoe from one to the other).

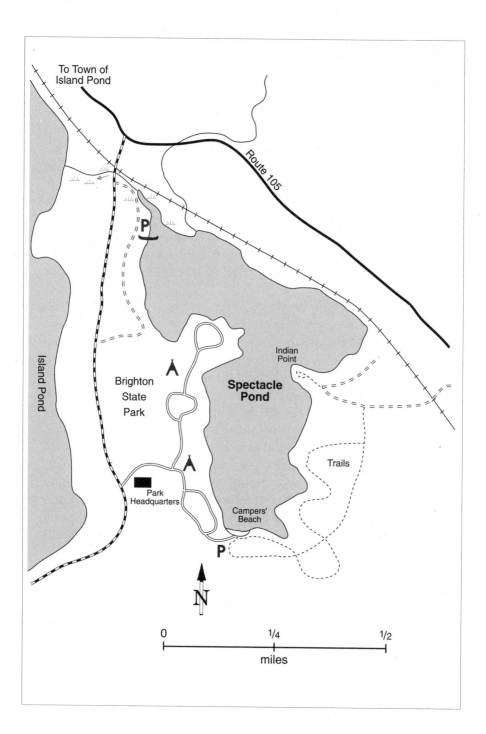

To Town of
Island Pond

Route 105

Island Pond

P

Brighton
State
Park

Spectacle
Pond

Indian
Point

Trails

Park
Headquarters

Campers'
Beach

P

N

0		1/4		1/2

miles

There are a few houses on Spectacle Pond, primarily at the north-western end, and railroad tracks pass along the northeastern shore. Spectacle Pond isn't the wildest of places in the Northeast Kingdom, but it is very attractive, and Brighton State Park is a great place for family camping. The pond and camping area are centrally located and provide a base from which to explore the other fine canoeing spots in this region (see sections on Norton Pond, Little Averill Pond, Holland Pond, Lake Willoughby, and May Pond).

GETTING THERE: To get to Spectacle Pond, turn south off Route 105 about a mile east of the town of Island Pond, and follow signs to Brighton State Park. For information or camping reservations, contact Brighton State Park, P.O. Box 413, Island Pond, VT 05846; 802-723-4360.

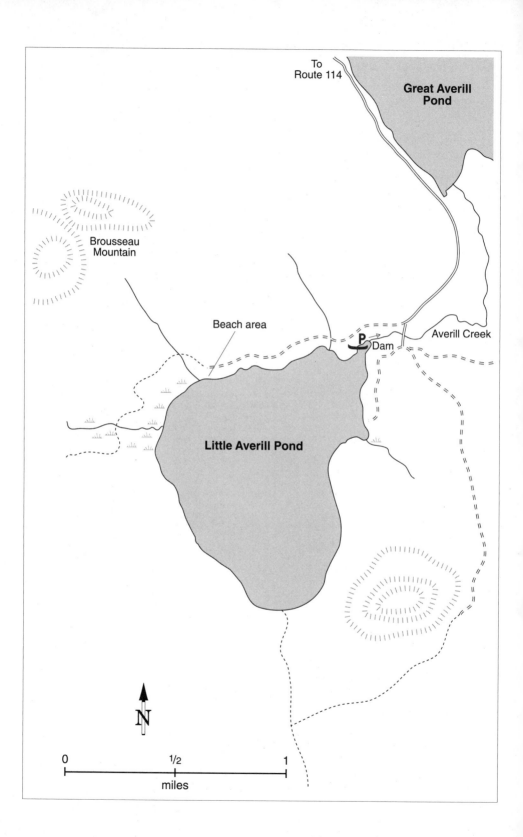

To
Route 114

**Great Averill
Pond**

Brousseau
Mountain

Beach area

P

Dam

Averill Creek

Little Averill Pond

N

0   1/2   1
miles

Little Averill Pond
Averill, VT

Little Averill Pond lies just south of the Canadian border in the Northeast Kingdom of Vermont. Like its larger brother to the north, Great Averill Pond, Little Averill is situated in deep boreal forest composed of spruce, fir, cedar, red maple, white birch, and yellow birch. Beautiful Brousseau Mountain, with an extensive cliff area, overlooks the pond from the northwest. There is some development around the pond, though much less than you will find at Great Averill.

Little Averill is a round, deep pond of 483 acres that boasts excellent fishing for lake, rainbow and brook trout. (Great Averill Pond also has landlocked salmon.) The shore is densely wooded and generally rocky, though there are a few sandy beaches. The Nature Conservancy has purchased a tract of land in the northwestern part of the pond, including a deep inlet, to protect loon nesting habitat. The inlet is exquisite, with wispy horsetails and grasses growing in the water amid the whitened snags of long-dead trees. From May through July, however, this area is generally off-limits to paddlers, as it is used by loons for nesting. On the northern shore of the pond is a large sandy beach area.

GETTING THERE: There is a state fishing access to the pond at the northeastern tip, next to the dam. You can reach it from a dirt road off Route 114. Coming from the west, pick up Route 114 East in Norton, where Route 147 comes in from Canada (just below Customs). Continue east on Route 114 for 3.4 miles to an unmarked gravel road on the right. Turn here and drive generally southeast along Great Averill Pond for 3.0 miles. Take the right fork and continue another 0.2 mile to the

Nestled beneath the cliffs of Brousseau Mountain and surrounded by deep boreal forests, Little Averill Pond has a real wilderness feel to it.

dam and the boat access. If you're coming from the east, the dirt road turns off Route 114 1.0 mile west of the Lakeview Store, which is near the fishing access to Great Averill Pond.

There is an outhouse at the fishing access, but camping is not permitted (see the section on Spectacle Pond for a camping location in this general area). A trail extends from Little Averill Pond west from the boat access around the northern end of the pond and goes south to the Black Branch of the Nulhegan River and northwest toward Norton. Another trail extends south from the southern tip of the pond along the East Branch of the Nulhegan River (see the *Vermont Atlas and Gazetteer*).

Holland Pond
Holland, VT

Less than a mile as the crow flies from the Canadian border in the Northeast Kingdom sits Holland Pond. The 334-acre pond is moderately developed along its western shore (approximately forty cottages), but these summer cottages are much different from the ones farther south. There aren't big docks and huge motorboats looming in front of every house, and there doesn't seem to be any new development. These are small, unpretentious camps, and though the pond would be much nicer if it were totally undeveloped, it's still a nice place to visit.

From the paddler's perspective, both the northern and southern ends are more exciting than the rest of the pond. There are two inlets at the southern end as well as a fairly extensive marshy area. You can explore these inlets a little amid the alders and sphagnum- and grass-covered tussocks, but you can't paddle in very far. And during the loon nesting season (May through July) you may not be able to canoe in this marshy area at all. (On many lakes and ponds with nesting loons, including Holland Pond, concerned individuals and/or organizations involved with loon protection will rope off the immediate area where loons are nesting and put up warning signs.) A few of the cottages are quite close to the south end.

The northern end of the pond feels a little more remote and wild. You can paddle into the northeast inlet a little ways, and if you feel really adventurous, you can carry your boat from here a couple of hundred yards into Turtle Pond, which is totally remote. The trail to Turtle Pond is on the northwestern side of the inlet, where the inlet narrows to a rock-strewn channel. Judging from the tracks on the trail, it is maintained primarily by moose, not people. Turtle Pond is very small but beautiful.

Farther around the northern end of Holland Pond to the east there are two nice picnic spots: one on a large flattish rock protruding into the pond, and another where the other inlet creek flows in. Here the small creek flows over huge, flat rocks beneath a stand of large northern white cedars. You may find trails here to several other small ponds to the north. Most of the rest of the pond's shoreline is quite densely grown with cedar, balsam fir, larch, white and yellow birch, and red spruce.

GETTING THERE: Holland Pond is not on the way to anywhere but Holland Pond, which is one reason it isn't too well known. If you're

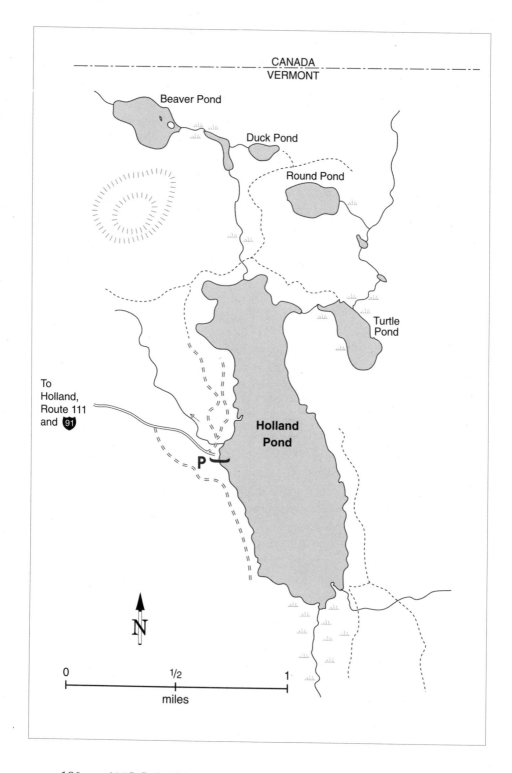

CANADA

VERMONT

Beaver Pond

Duck Pond

Round Pond

Turtle Pond

To
Holland,
Route 111
and 91

Holland
Pond

P

N

0   1/2   1

miles

coming north on I-91, get off at Exit 29 (right at the Canadian border) and turn onto the paved road toward Holland and Morgan Center (initially this road runs along the border). After passing Holland Elementary School on the left, keep an eye out for a dirt road on the left. The turnoff is 5.3 miles from I-91, just as the paved road curves to the right. Follow this dirt road for 5.3 miles to the pond (bear to the right at 3.0 miles and bear left at 5.0 miles, staying on the main road). If you're driving from the southeast on Route 111, turn north onto a paved road at the north end of Seymore Lake by the large public parking area and Seymore Lake Lodge. Go 4.7 miles on this road and turn right onto a dirt road as the paved road curves to the left. Follow directions to the pond as above.

There is no camping at Holland Pond, but Brighton State Park on Spectacle Pond is only about twenty miles away (see section on Spectacle Pond). Fishing for brook and rainbow trout is pretty good in Holland Pond.

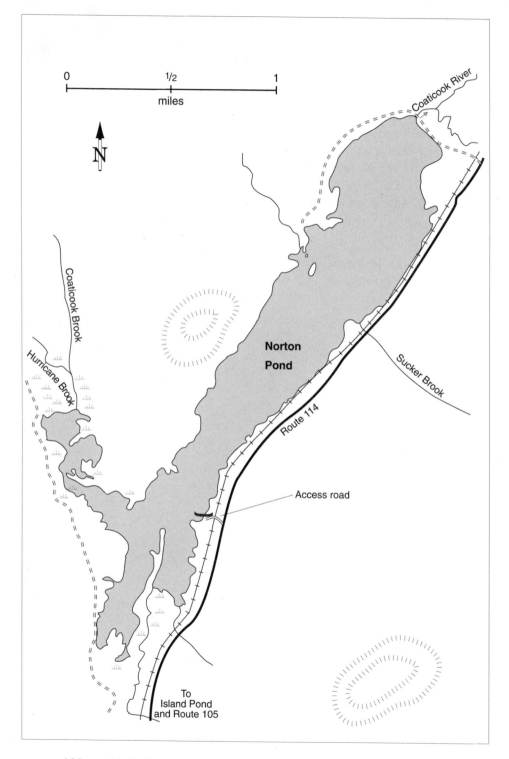

Norton Pond

Warren Gore, Norton, VT

Norton Pond isn't as well known as the Averill Ponds, Lake Willoughby, and some of the other lakes and ponds in the Northeast Kingdom of Vermont. But for the paddler, Norton has some real advantages. Although there is some development at the northern end, near the center on the western shore, and at the southernmost extension, the pond is quite long, with many more coves and inlets for the paddler to explore. The entire southern end of the 583-acre pond is filled with islands, deep coves, and long, winding inlet brooks.

While canoeing the northern extension of Norton Pond is pleasant, I much prefer the southern end and especially the marshy inlet to the northwest, where Hurricane Brook and Coaticook Brook flow in. There are no houses here, and it's a great area for wildlife: wood ducks, black ducks, herons, deer, and moose (judging from the tracks along the swampy shores, I'd say that this is a favorite grazing area for moose). Even in the late summer, when the water level is down and the pond vegetation at a peak, you can paddle quite far up these creeks. With higher water in late spring, the area is much more accessible. Where this northwest extension joins the main pond, there are a number of different channels through and around the various islands to explore. At the far southern end you'll find some gorgeous little coves and just a few summer cottages.

GETTING THERE: Access to Norton Pond is from a state fishing access just off Route 114 near the southern end of the pond. Coming from the south, the access road is 9.0 miles north of the intersection with Route 105 at Island Pond. From the north, the access is 7.3 miles from Route 147 at the Canadian border. Turn off Route 114 to the west onto a dirt road. This access road initially heads north, then crosses the railroad tracks and curves more to the south. The state fishing access is about one-quarter mile from Route 114. There is an outhouse at the access.

The Great Blue Heron
Professor of the Marsh

Somehow the great blue heron always reminds me of a professor. The stately, long-legged bird stands in the shallows as if quietly contemplating life, its plumage looking a bit like a three-piece suit—gray and usually rumpled as the bird fishes for breakfast. Flying, the wing beats are slow and graceful, never rushed.

The great blue heron, *Ardea herodias,* is the largest bird you will regularly encounter on our lakes and ponds. Adults stand four feet high and have a wingspan of six feet. Males and females are indistinguishable from one another, but you can distinguish between adults and juveniles—only adults have white on the top of the head.

Physically, the great blue heron provides a fascinating contrast with another bird you'll probably encounter on your excursions: the loon (see page 51). The heron is far larger than the loon, yet weighs about the same or a little less. Loons are adapted to diving and swimming underwater, while herons need long legs for wading. To avoid damage to its delicate legs, a heron must alight very softly. The heron has almost four times the wing area per unit of body weight than the loon; these large wings allow it to take off easily and soar to a gentle landing. Loons, by contrast, must flap their wings very rapidly, and hovering is out of the question.

Great blue herons nest in rookeries with dozens or even hundreds of other pairs. Some rookeries have been occupied for decades, such as the large one at Missisquoi Wildlife Refuge in the northwestern corner of Vermont (see page 197). Nests are usually built near the tops of tall trees. The ideal site for a rookery is a swamp where the trees are surrounded by water for added protection from predators, such as raccoons. But a rookery won't last forever; excrement from the birds usually kills the trees after a long period of occupation.

Eggs are laid in the spring, and both parents share the duties of incubation, hatching three to five young after about a month. Because herons begin incubating their eggs before all of them are laid, the young hatch over a period of up to a week. This results in some young being larger than others. If food is in short supply, the smaller young often won't survive. The smaller birds may even be pushed from the nest by their siblings.

If you happen to paddle near a rookery in the spring, you will definitely know it. There is a cacophony of loud croaking and the *kak-kak-kak* of young calling to their parents returning with food. If you get close you will smell the stench of rotting fish, excrement, and, often, dead herons beneath the rookery. If you get too close you may become familiar with the bird's unpleasant defense: regurgitating partially digested fish on their intruders.

Most of the great blue herons you'll see while canoeing will be feeding at the edge of lakes or ponds. They stand perfectly still in the water or on a tussock of grass by the water's edge, waiting for an unsuspecting fish, frog, salamander, or other prey to come into range. Then they strike out with lightning speed, usually using their long bill like forceps to catch the prey, but occasionally spearing it (perhaps by mistake). In the fall herons migrate from New England down the coast to a location where fishing is possible throughout the winter.

Great blue herons and their long-legged cousins, the egrets, were almost exterminated by hunting in the late 1800s. Their long feathers were prized for hat-making. The near-demise of these species helped spur interest in conservation and led to passage of laws in the early 1900s fully protecting herons. Today, great blue heron populations are strong, but the bird is still considered at risk, as wetland habitat continues to be destroyed.

South Bay, Lake Memphremagog
Newport, VT

The South Bay of Lake Memphremagog is an interesting body of water, and much more appropriate for canoeing than Lake Memphremagog proper. At the northern end, in the city of Newport, South Bay feels quite urban. You can hear sirens, trucks, heavy equipment, and cars on the nearby streets. But as you paddle farther south and into a long sinewy channel extending three or four miles, most of that noise fades away.

There is a state fishing access on the western shore of South Bay not too far from the northern end. Paddling south from here, the water is quite open for a ways. You can paddle up the meandering Black River, which flows into South Bay about a quarter-mile below the fishing access. Parts of the river are lined with silver maples and willows dipping their lowest branches into the water, and other stretches are marsh. The river has a rather industrial feel to it—like some rivers I've paddled on in Rhode Island, where mysterious seepages from landfills and abandoned industrial plants drip into the smelly water—but Black River is very clean, not at all like those Rhode Island industrial rivers.

As you paddle farther south on South Bay, the open water disappears into thick marshes of pickerelweed, waterlilies, watershield, rushes, sedges, grasses, and cattails. In fact, most of the southern part of the bay is not even canoeable. Paddling through the marshy islands, you may find yourself in the channel of the Barton River. This is another winding, slow-moving river lined with silver maples, but here you are a lot farther from the city. There are many signs of beaver, and you're much more likely to see wood ducks than pigeons.

Curiously, the Barton River roughly parallels another, much wider, channel leading to the south. Either one can be followed south through the South Bay State Wildlife Management Area (a portion of which has been protected by the Vermont Nature Conservancy). This is one of the few sites in Vermont where black terns nest. I haven't been far on the Barton River, but I have paddled quite a ways down the more eastern channel. To get to this channel from the Barton River, you may have to paddle back to the main lake and then north a bit; the marshes are so varied and changing that it's hard to give precise directions. But you should recognize this other, unnamed, channel when you get to it. It's quite wide and relatively deep, lined with marsh plants and home to a wide assortment of water birds. Fairly soon after getting into the channel you will pass under the railroad bridge (be aware that some of the

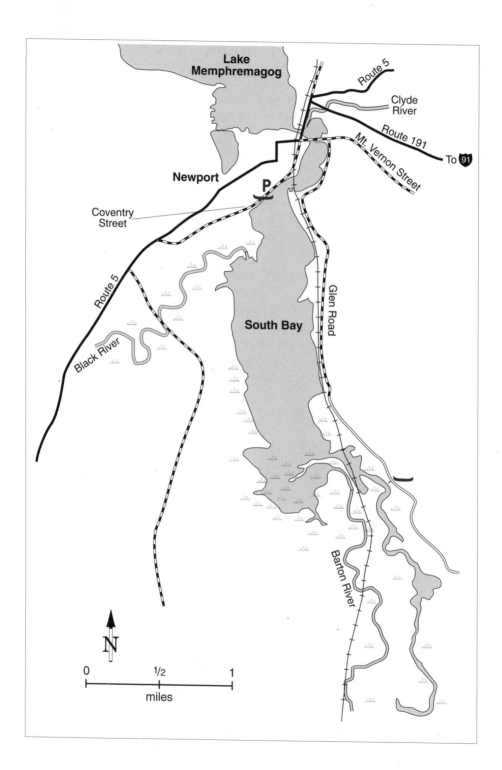

older wooden posts holding up the trestle have been cut off at or just below water level—take it slowly paddling through).

From the railroad bridge, you can paddle several miles south through increasingly beautiful country. I was pressed for time when paddling here, but I couldn't bring myself to turn around. I kept telling myself, "Just one more bend to see what's ahead," until I had gotten to the southern end, where passage was blocked by vegetation. By then the sun had almost dipped to the horizon and I had to beat a hasty retreat back to the fishing access, five or six miles away. You'll see lots of wood-duck nesting boxes—and lots of the results. I've never seen as many wood ducks in one place as I saw along the winding channels of South Bay. I must have seen a hundred, mostly in groups of a half-dozen or so (it was late enough in the season that the year's young had taken wing). I also saw bitterns, black ducks, kingfishers, great blue herons, a marsh hawk, lots of painted turtles, and a few snapping turtles—just the triangular nose sticking up above the water (see page 89 for more on this curious beast). Feathery larches mix with the silver maples, white birch, spruce, and other trees along the shores.

Time your visit to South Bay carefully. The area is used for duck hunting in the fall, as evidenced by the duck blinds hidden among the marsh plants. As with other lakes, ponds, and rivers where duck hunting is common, I recommend avoiding this place during duck hunting season. Contact the Vermont Fish and Wildlife Department for hunting season dates (103 South Main St., Waterbury, VT 05676; 802-244-7331).

GETTING THERE: To reach the state fishing access, get off I-91 at Exit 27 and take Route 191 West to Route 5 South. After crossing the bridge between South Bay and Lake Memphremagog, turn left onto Coventry Street and follow the water down to the boat access on the left, about a half-mile from where you turn off Route 5.

There is also an unmarked access to the southern inlet of South Bay just south of the railroad trestle. This is on Glen Road, which you reach by driving around the northern tip of South Bay on Coventry Street and Mt. Vernon Street. Follow Glen Road down the eastern side, keeping as close to the water as you can. From the turn onto Glen Road drive 2.7 miles south (the road turns to dirt after 2.4 miles). You will see a little dirt track leading down to the water on the right.

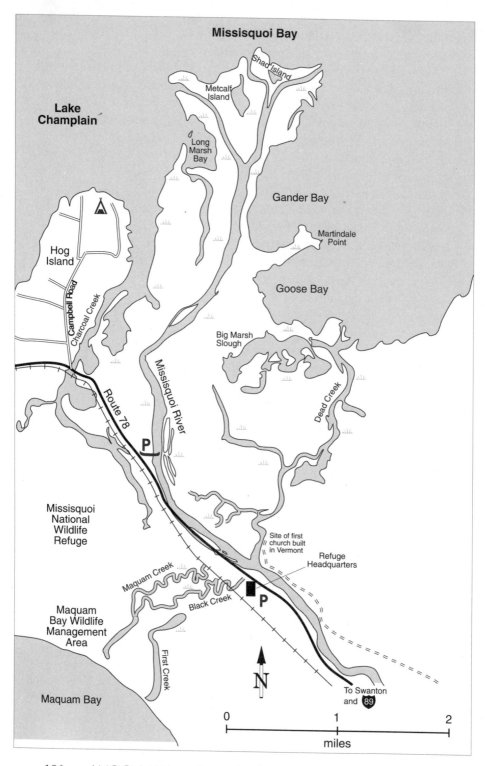

Missisquoi Bay

Shad Island

Metcalf Island

Lake Champlain

Long Marsh Bay

Gander Bay

Martindale Point

Hog Island

Campbell Road

Charcoal Creek

Goose Bay

Missisquoi River

Big Marsh Slough

Dead Creek

P

Route 78

Missisquoi National Wildlife Refuge

Site of first church built in Vermont

Refuge Headquarters

Maquam Creek

Black Creek

P

Maquam Bay Wildlife Management Area

First Creek

N

To Swanton and 89

Maquam Bay

0   1   2

miles

Missisquoi Delta, Lake Champlain

Highgate, VT

Lake Champlain, for the most part, is not the sort of lake that belongs in a guide to quiet water canoeing. Even a relatively light wind (five to ten miles per hour) can produce swells of a foot or more, and a breeze over fifteen MPH can produce dangerous whitecaps and virtually uncanoeable water. But that doesn't mean the lake should be totally off-limits, either. There are a few places on the lake that, under the right conditions, are very appropriate for the open-boat paddler, including Missisquoi Bay and the delta of the Missisquoi River (see also the section in Lake Champlain–Southern End, page 120).

Way up in the northwestern corner of Vermont, virtually a stone's throw from the Canadian line, sits the Missisquoi National Wildlife Refuge and within it some very enjoyable boating. The Abanaki word Missisquoi means "great grassy meadow." Over the years, at least twenty different spellings of the word have appeared. In the Missisquoi Delta there are basically two canoeable channels: Missisquoi River proper, which divides into several different branches near its terminus, and Dead Creek, which branches off the Missisquoi near the headquarters of the Missisquoi National Wildlife Refuge. Most of the other bays and inlets in the refuge are off-limits during spring and summer to protect waterfowl nesting sites and one of the only osprey nesting sites in Vermont. Be sure to follow these rules to avoid harming the numerous nesting species.

On a calm day, you can make a nice loop of these channels. From the main boat landing on Route 78, paddle downstream along the Missisquoi River, then around the eastern side of the peninsula and up Dead Creek to its intersection with the Missisquoi and back to the boat landing. The trip could just as well be made in the opposite direction. On Shad Island you will see several hundred large nests up in the trees. This is a great blue heron rookery, one of the largest around, to which herons travel many miles to nest. During spring and early summer, the loud croaking from a heron rookery is quite something (see page 190 for more on this curious species). You're also likely to see cormorants off the Shad Island point and both black and common terns flying around Lake Champlain (Missisquoi has one of the largest nesting populations of black terns in New England, and it is one of the only places in Vermont where you can see the threatened common tern. Missisquoi is also one of the only places in Vermont where soft-shelled turtles are found.)

The thick silver maple swamps lend an eerie feeling to the Missisquoi River where it flows into Lake Champlain.

Fishing is popular in the Missisquoi Refuge, especially for walleye along the Missisquoi River. Other fish caught here include muskellunge, northern pike, catfish, pickerel, horned pout, black crappie, largemouth and smallmouth bass, yellow perch, and landlocked salmon.

While there may be quite a few motorboats on the Missisquoi River on a busy weekend, Dead Creek is likely to be much quieter. On a windless May afternoon we watched a mink along the bank of Dead Creek—or I should say the mink watched us. (Mink are such curious animals that if you catch a glimpse of one, be patient. It will quite likely reappear for another look at you.) Nearby we watched a deer splash through the shallow water. Because the refuge is used heavily for duck hunting in the fall, you will do well to keep away from here during waterfowl hunting seasons—check the dates with the Missisquoi Wildlife Refuge (802-865-4781) or the Vermont Fish and Wildlife Department, 103 South Main St., Waterbury, VT 05676; 802-244-7331.

Silver maple is the dominant tree along the Missisquoi River and Dead Creek. With many of the maples growing right out of the water, it reminds me of a Louisiana cypress swamp. Out near Lake Champlain there are a few places where you can actually paddle through these trees, weaving a twisted course and encountering an occasional wood duck. Be sure not to canoe in restricted areas, though—most of the thick silver maple swamps are off-limits. The restricted areas are clearly marked with signs.

Along with canoeing, you might want to hike on some of the trails. Two short trails leave from park headquarters and pass along Black Creek and Maquam Creek, covering roughly 1.5 miles. A brochure is available at the Refuge headquarters that includes descriptions of what you are likely to see. Just across from the Refuge headquarters where Dead Creek splits off from the Missisquoi River is the site of the first church in Vermont.

GETTING THERE: Missisquoi is easily accessible, just a few miles from Interstate 89. Get off the interstate at Exit 21 and take Route 78 West. The Missisquoi National Wildlife Refuge Headquarters is on the left approximately 3.0 miles from I-89, through the town of Swanton. Stop here to pick up a map of the refuge and find out which areas are restricted. The refuge also has brochures on birds, mammals, hiking trails, and fishing.

There is no camping in the refuge, but there are a few private campgrounds in the area. The closest, Cambell's Bay Campground on Hog Island (just across from the refuge), is mainly for trailer camping, and many of those are seasonal trailers. You can find other camping areas in the *Vermont Atlas and Gazetteer* or a state highway map. For more information, contact the Missisquoi National Wildlife Refuge, RFD 2, Swanton, VT 05488; 802-868-4781.

Alphabetical Listing of Lakes and Ponds

New Hampshire

Vermont